Becoming a
Customer-Focused
Organization

Becoming a Customer-Focused Organization

Craig Cochran

Foreword by Michael Coles
President and CEO, Caribou Coffee Co. Inc.

Preface by Chuck Bengochea
President, HoneyBaked Ham Co. of Georgia

Afterword by Danny Helmly
President and CEO, BellSouth Communication Systems, LLC

Paton Press LLC
Chico, California

9/06
Don

Most Paton Press books are available at quantity discounts when purchased in bulk. For more information, contact:

Paton Press LLC
P.O. Box 44
Chico, CA 95927-0044
Telephone: (530) 342-5480
Fax: (530) 342-5471
E-mail: books@patonpress.com
Web: www.patonpress.com

10 09 08 07 06 05 5 4 3 2 1

ISBN-13: 978-1-932828-05-4
ISBN-10: 1-932828-05-2

Library of Congress Cataloging-in-Publication Data

Cochran, Craig, 1964-
  Becoming a customer-focused organization / Craig Cochran; foreword by
Michael Coles, afterword by Danny Helmly.
     p. cm.
  ISBN 1-932828-05-2
  1. Customer relations. I. Title.
  HF5415.5.C58 2006
  658.8'12—dc22
                    2005029500

Staff
Publisher: Scott M. Paton
Editor: Taran March
Book design: David Hurst

Dedicated to Granny, Thelma O'Dell.

You don't build it for yourself.
You know what the people want, and you build it for them.
—Walt Disney

Contents

Foreword

I've been in the retail business all of my life. My career began when I was eleven years old. Throughout the course of my lifetime, I've learned many valuable lessons; however, the most important one I ever learned happened shortly after my career began.

I was working for a man named Irving Settler. Irving owned a young men's clothing store. It was "the" store of the time. One day, about two years after my career with him began, I was cleaning up the store, which was a total mess after the single biggest day in the store's history. I was straightening piles of slacks, refolding shirts, and hanging suits and sport jackets back onto the rack. After several hours of hard work, the store was finally back in order and we were about to end what had turned into a fourteen-hour workday. As we were leaving, I turned to Irving and said, "What a great day! These customers love us. We own them!" He turned to me and said, "Kid, the minute you think that you own any one of your customers, you're dead! You might as well close up shop right then and there. Always remember that there are fifty people standing in the wings waiting to take your customers and your business away from you."

The lesson stuck.

Becoming a customer-focused organization isn't a clever catchphrase, nor is it a fad that will fall in and out of style. Putting a customer at the forefront of the business has been around since people were making purchases with salt. Today it's become one of the great differentiators of retail business. So many companies have lost their way. Companies that "get it" move to the front of their group. It's one of the things a business must do to continue to thrive and survive.

In a world of ninety-day financial reporting where every detail of the company's results is measured, the customer doesn't appear on any balance sheet and is rarely taken into account. Financial performance is an important measure of a company's health and well being, but it's the customer that keeps the business's heart beating. Craig Cochran's book is a remarkable road map to help create this important culture shift inside an organization.

—Michael Coles
Co-founder, Great American Cookie Co.
Current president and CEO of Caribou Coffee Co. Inc.

Preface

I recently finished reading Craig's book, *Becoming a Customer-Focused Organization,* and greatly enjoyed it. The book provides a lot of practical guidance and tools, but most important, it forced me to challenge my assumption that we're a customer-focused organization. I'm president of The HoneyBaked Ham Co. of Georgia. Our company has been in business since 1973 and has very strong brand awareness and loyal customer following. Those facts, however, don't guarantee future success.

Today's consumers lead fast-paced lives and are focused on making smart purchasing decisions. They don't have time for mistakes. Our company delivers the world's best ham, but, truthfully, we can be inconvenient to get to, and we're premium-priced. For the consumer to continue to visit our stores when there are so many alternatives, we must deliver excellence in product quality and customer service. Customers must be delighted by their visits and compelled to go out of their way and visit again.

Craig's book challenged me to consider customer service in a broader context and focus on process and simplicity. The first challenge was to acknowledge that our organization from top to bottom wasn't as customer-focused as it should be. The leadership team wasn't actively engaged in customer service issues and, frankly, not sufficiently discussing or measuring customer service. We've made changes to correct that. Second, Craig's book challenged us to create simple processes to capture and leverage customer information. As he says, a customer complaint is an urgent call from a trusted source. We're in the process of building that information loop to ensure that all customer feedback is appropriately reviewed and acted on. Both challenges have been extremely helpful because we've focused the entire organization on the importance of truly transforming our service culture and service experience.

Our service philosophy is to "earn our customers' trust with every visit." The idea is that we should never take our customers for granted. Every visit should delight them with the product and the experience. I'm convinced that a top-to-bottom. relentless focus on customer service is critical to earning that trust and ensuring long-term brand health. I appreciate Craig's book and his customer service message. He's right on!

—Chuck Bengochea
President, HoneyBaked Ham Co. of Georgia

Acknowledgments

I'd like to offer my special thanks to the following people and organizations for their assistance in the development of this book: Muriel, Brynn, and Cullen Cochran; P.C. and Linda Cochran; Dr. Brett Saks, Kim Saks, and Aaron Saks—Dynamic Chiropractic & Acupuncture Clinics, PC (Chandler, AZ); John and Rocio Lancaster; Thelma O'Dell; Michael J. Coles and Jami Smith—Caribou Coffee (Minneapolis, MN); Dale Griffin—Yokogawa Corp. of America (Newnan, GA); Chuck Bengochea, Kathy Laggis, and Greg Hundt—HoneyBaked Hams of Georgia (Atlanta, GA); Danny Helmly, Kevin A. Machell-Cox, David Dragan—Bellsouth Communication Systems, LLC (Atlanta, GA); Rosemarie Kobau—Centers for Disease Control and Prevention (Atlanta, GA); John Thomas (Marietta, GA); Lee Crayfish Coursey (Atlanta, GA); Paolo Chiappina, Stephen Dockham—Sara Lee Inc. (Winston-Salem, NC); the entire staff of Georgia Tech's Economic Development Institute (Atlanta, GA); Marc Timothy Smith—Cayman Business Systems (West Chester, Ohio); the contributors and moderators of Marc Smith's Elsmar Cove Forums (*http://elsmar.com/Forums/index.php*); Scott Paton, Heidi Paton, Taran March, Christel Whetstone, and Anna Moss—Paton Press (Chico, CA); Dirk Dusharme, Robert Green, Caylen Balmain, Mike Richman, Laurel Thoennes—*Quality Digest* (Chico, CA, *www.qualitydigest.com*); Sue Renda—Coca-Cola North America (Lehigh Valley, PA); Ted Barber, Deborah Holden, Lloyd Snively, Peter C. Chatel, Troy Clarida, Ann Barrelle, Michon Mitchell, and Lynn Ann Pall—The Coca-Cola Co. (Atlanta, GA); John Saccheri—Mystique Shopper LLC (Orlando, FL); Michael Stamp—SI Corp. (Chickamauga, GA); Mauren Lovell, Steven Maskell—Shop'n Chek Worldwide (Norcross, GA); Thomas G. Loebig—Ension Inc. (Pittsburgh, PA); Dr. L. Ramakrishnan—Philips Electronics (Pune, India); Claes Gefvenberg (Eskilstuna, Sweden); Wallace Tait (Ontario, Canada); Greg Baker—Queensland Magnesia Pty Ltd (Rockhampton, Queensland, Australia); Simon Temperley–SaferPak

Ltd. (Manchester, England); Bill Ryan (Madison, WI); Jim Howe—JRB Co. (Akron, OH); Wes Bucey (Libertyville, IL); Craig Hollingsworth—Burgess Pigment Co. (Sandersville, GA); Robb Nix—Merritech (Saginaw, MI); Jodi L. Medley-McMahon—Flex Quality Solutions LLC (Milwaukee, WI); Govindarajan Ramu—JDS Uniphase Corp. (San Jose, CA); Larry Whittington—Whittington Associates (Atlanta, GA); Susan VanHemert—Simple Harmony Computing Services Inc. (Kennesaw, GA); John E. Gray—Air Combat Command, Program Management Squadron, U.S. Air Force (Newport News, VA); Lauren Kelly—CVS/Pharmacy (Woonsocket, RI); and Patty Romeo—Totem Ocean Trailer Express, Inc. (Tacoma, WA).

CHAPTER 1

The Customer Focus Inventory

Everybody talks about the importance of being customer-focused. "Keep your eyes on the customer!" urge most organizational mantras. So much is said, in fact, that the underlying reality of these words often gets lost. Of course, everyone must keep his or her eyes on the customer. The customer is the sole reason organizations exist.

That statement bears repeating:

The customer is the sole reason organizations exist.

Before you start quibbling with my logic, consider that all organizations have customers of some sort. Businesses have customers who purchase goods and services. Charities have customers who receive their charity and other customers who make the charity possible. Churches have customers who want to nurture their faith. Schools have customers who want to learn. Governments have customers who expect good decisions and efficient services for their tax dollars. Law enforcement agencies have customers who want to be safe and secure. Clubs have customers who seek fellowship with like-minded people. All organizations have customers, and they're the sole reason the organizations exist.

However, the customer focus can waver when you consider the second essential reality of organizations: They're composed of people, and people are remarkably good at self-preservation. Once someone becomes part of an organization, it's only natural to want to remain a part of it (at least until something better comes along). Given the desire for self-preservation, everybody's focus eventually begins to turn inward. Instead of looking outward at the customer, members of the organization become preoccupied with internal processes and procedures that give meaning to each person's work. At that point, the organization stops being about its customers and starts being about the organizational members and their survival.

The irony is that this inward orientation doesn't ensure survival. In fact, it guarantees the opposite: irrelevance, obsolescence, and death. Too much inward focus will ensure that the organization is replaced by a competitor. "But my organization doesn't have any competitors!" you object. If you believe that, you're crazy. Just as every organization has customers, it also has competitors. Even governments have competitors.

We've come to three fundamental realizations during this short lesson about organizations:

- All organizations have customers.
- Organizations have a natural tendency to turn inward and stop focusing on their customers.
- All organizations have competitors that will happily replace them when they stop focusing on customers.

If you believe these facts, then you must also believe that customer focus has the most bearing on your organization's survival and success. Not focusing on the customer guarantees that someone else will. Then it's only a matter of time before someone puts padlocks on your doors.

KEY PROCESSES FOR
STAYING CUSTOMER FOCUSED

Customer focus requires effort and discipline on a daily basis. It's a process that continues for as long as the organization hopes to exist. Just when you think your organization has achieved a degree of customer focus, evidence appears that indicates quite the opposite. However, just realizing that your organization lacks customer focus puts you miles ahead of most people. That realization alone is a significant breakthrough. Plenty of organizations still deny they even have customers, let alone that they lack a customer focus.

A number of key processes will help ensure a customer focus. Each of these is described in subsequent chapters of this book, but we'll discuss them briefly here:

■ *Management systems.* Building a management system around the customer's needs makes perfect sense, but it's often neglected. Establish a system that uses only as many procedures and processes as are absolutely necessary. Each process should be directly linked to a customer.

■ *Innovation.* Customers want goods and services that are continually improving. Innovation is the process that drives these improvements, and it must be carefully monitored and controlled.

■ *Training.* Training is a critical tool for helping employees maintain a customer focus. The training program should be designed with the customer in mind, and it should strengthen competencies that produce customer satisfaction and customer loyalty.

■ *Leadership and culture.* Every organization has a culture that influences its members. The organization must develop a culture that reinforces and rewards customer focus. This culture starts with the leadership of the organization.

■ *Customer perceptions.* Effective gauges of customer perceptions are among the most important tools in the organization. The leaner and simpler the tools, the better. After learning about customer perceptions, the organization must make sure it can act on what it learns.

■ *Complaint resolution.* As inevitable as the sun rising every morning, customers will complain. The organization should consider itself lucky when a customer goes to the trouble of complaining. A complaint provides one more opportunity for the organization to shine.

All these concepts seem simple enough. In fact, most managers would argue that their organizations have these issues well in hand. But do they really? Are the organization's personnel truly focused on the customer? Are systems established that reinforce this focus? Do all employees really understand the effect they have on their organization's reason for existence? Probably not.

ESTABLISHING A BASELINE
FOR IMPROVEMENT

Organizations need a tool that provides quantitative proof of where they really stand in relation to customer focus. This tool, called the customer focus inventory, appears in appendix A. The inventory is composed of fifty statements, each followed by a five-point scale ranging from strongly disagree to strongly agree. The customer focus inventory is a self-diagnostic tool that's used by employees on their own organization. The gaps that emerge from the inventory become action items in the organization's improvement plans.

Each statement on the customer focus inventory requires a scaled response, which in turn produces a score:

RESPONSE	SCORE
Strongly disagree	-2
Disagree	-1
Neutral	0
Agree	+1
Strongly agree	+2

The highest score an organization can receive on the inventory is 100. Most organizations score considerably lower. In fact, scores of below 50 are quite common. That's OK because becoming customer focused is a continual process, and recognition is the first step. To improve its score, the organization targets in its improvement plans the gaps revealed by the customer focus inventory.

The customer focus inventory is intended to be a recurring process. At the beginning of the customer-focus effort, it's helpful to set a baseline of where the organization stands. As the organization becomes more sophisticated, the customer focus score should improve to reflect the changes that have been made. The inventory becomes a changing gauge of how well the organization is focused on its reason for existence.

Using the customer focus inventory is simple and intuitive:

1. Assemble a diverse group of organizational members. Limit the group to 8–10 participants because the interaction can quickly become unmanageable.

2. Assign a facilitator to the group. The facilitator will ensure the group stays focused and manage any conflict that arises. This person must also make sure that no single person dominates discussion. The risk of this happening is especially strong when a powerful and persuasive chief executive is present.

3. Read each statement on the customer focus inventory and agree on a consensus response. Discourage the group from becoming too preoccupied with the subtle differences between responses (for instance, "agree" versus "strongly agree"). The group's first reaction will probably be the most accurate response. Where the group can't come to consensus, strive for a compromise response.

4. Tabulate the total scores for the inventory. This is the organization's baseline on which it will work to improve.

5. Examine the completed inventory for statements that received a response of "disagree" or "strongly disagree." These represent special opportunities for the organization to sharpen its focus on the customer.

Is it possible to perform well on the customer focus inventory and still not produce customer satisfaction and loyalty? Of course. The inventory is only a measurement tool, and a subjective one at that. Its most significant weakness is that it uses internal perceptions of how customer focused the organization is. The true gauges of focus are the customers themselves, who hold the success of your organization in their hands. The customer focus inventory is a good start on the journey toward true customer focus. The rest of this book will provide specific guidelines and tools for facilitating your progress.

CHAPTER 2

Leadership Drives
Customer Focus

C ustomer focus doesn't evolve on its own. It's carefully cultivated over time through a variety of processes. The organization's leadership is responsible for making customer focus a theme that affects every decision that's made and every action that's taken. Customer focus can't be delegated to lower levels in the organization. It must start at the top and be refreshed from the top at regular intervals. When organizations fail to achieve customer focus, it's usually because their leaders were never properly engaged in the process. In other words, top management failed to lead.

Leaders must acknowledge a number of realities about customer focus. These are fundamentals that should reside at the top of a leader's to-do list. Let's examine each one and discuss how top management can deliver on one of its most important duties: driving customer focus.

CUSTOMER FOCUS IS
EVERY LEADER'S RESPONSIBILITY

A couple of years ago I spoke to the president of a company that was dealing with a huge customer complaint. Root cause analysis pointed to confusion about customer specifications in the finishing department. The company's liability was close to a million dollars. As expected, the president was very upset about the whole affair.

"Our finishing personnel failed the customer," he said grimly. "It's as simple as that."

The president became even more upset when I told him that he'd failed the customer.

All roads lead back to top management when we're talking about customer focus. An organization's leaders set the tone for everything that takes place: the good, the bad, and the ugly. Sure, top management didn't personally botch the customer's order, but its actions or inactions enabled others to botch the order.

Leaders, by definition, have followers. They might follow the leader to places he or she didn't intend or expect, so whatever the leader focuses on is of the utmost importance. When a leader focuses on issues other than the customer—such as turf battles, internal politics, and ego gratification—everyone else focuses on those issues and not the customer. The leader's interests are powerful beacons for the organization.

Let's explore some common customer service problems and how they relate to leadership:

- *Customers are offended by employees' attitudes.* Attitude is a function of the employees' environment. If it's cynical, negative, or demeaning, no one should be surprised that employees have bad attitudes. Top management has the single biggest effect on organizational environment, which means it also has the single biggest effect on attitude. Bad attitude equals poor leadership.

- *A poorly trained employee makes a mistake.* Training is one of the key processes for driving an awareness of customer requirements and expectations. Training also happens to be one of the least respected processes within organizations. Why? Because it's a soft process, one that's difficult to trace to return on investment. Leadership often views training as something that's nice to do when time allows, but not necessarily essential. It can be trimmed or cut entirely when business conditions dictate. Poorly trained employees are a sign that leadership isn't dedicated to improving and growing the organization over the long term.

- *Customers experience repeat problems.* Recurring problems that affect customers are the cancers of modern organizations. Most customers really don't mind isolated problems, errors, and mishaps. Of course, they'd prefer that every transaction is perfect, but most people will tolerate a problem here or there. This tolerance doesn't extend to repeat problems. One of top management's most critical jobs is to mobilize and focus the organization when threats appear on the horizon, and customer complaints are "code red" threats. When customers experience repeat problems, top management has failed to focus everyone on the organization's reason for existence.

■ *Customers find it difficult to communicate with the organization.* Communication is as vital to an organization as the bloodstream is to the body. When communication is blocked or slowed, it can have disastrous consequences. Leadership must provide the resources and encourage the awareness that enable communication with the customer on a variety of fronts. Obstructed communication means top management hasn't emphasized the importance of this critical process. Nothing is more important than communicating with your customers, and company leaders must make that fact clear to everyone.

These are but a handful of the hundreds of potential problems that have their roots in leadership. Top management must demonstrate clear customer focus in every job it carries out. Once top management achieves that focus, it must communicate it.

COMMUNICATING CUSTOMER FOCUS SHOULD BE TOP MANAGEMENT'S PRIORITY

Leaders are often referred to as the "mouthpieces" of their organizations. This characterization is quite apt. Leaders spend a considerable amount of time communicating. The communication usually covers many issues: strategic direction, opportunities, uncertainties, and achievements. Are customers ever mentioned? They certainly should be. In fact, customers should be talked about more than any other issue. The justifications for this are simple but critical:

■ Customers are the reason the organization exists.
■ The leader's roleis to keep the organization in existence.
■ The way to survive and thrive is to keep everyone focused on the customer.

Communication is the most common method leaders use to share their customer focus. Yes, actions are more powerful than words, but not everyone in the organization is privy to the leader's actions. However, everyone is exposed to the leader's words. The words carry the vision. When the leader's actions match his or her words, and both reveal a sharp focus on the customer, the organization's top-level vision aligns with its success.

Organizations have countless opportunities for communication, including telephone, e-mail, memos, meetings, teleconferences, and chat rooms. The medium isn't the problem; message content, frequency, and sincerity, however, often are. Fancy terms, but what do they really mean? Let's take a look:

- *Message content.* In all communication, the content of the message is the most fundamental issue. What's being communicated? The message must be clear and concise. There should be no doubt in anybody's mind what the organization should do regarding the customer. Fluffy platitudes aimed at inspiring people serve no purpose. Message content should follow the old *Dragnet* adage: "Just the facts, ma'am."

- *Frequency.* Employees must be regularly reminded of the reason for the organization's existence. It's easy to forget, especially because there's no shortage of distractions. Leadership should establish a regular conversation with the organization about its customers and their expectations.

- *Sincerity.* This relates back to action. Leaders must support their words with actions if they're sincere about the message. In fact, the message should include the details of actions that leaders have taken to drive customer focus. This grabs everyone's attention and leaves no doubt in anybody's mind as to whether leadership is serious.

Message content is a broad subject. What customer focus topics can leaders highlight in their communication? Here are a few ideas:

- *Customer service successes.* Where has the organization excelled in going above and beyond for the customer? Who was involved? What specific actions were taken? What was the customer's reaction? Unfortunately, in many organizations top management is far removed from customer service successes. Top managers must become involved because it's their job to communicate successes.

- *Recognition.* One of leadership's main communication jobs is to recognize individuals and teams that surpassed their job descriptions and truly delighted their customers. The trick is to identify where and when the exceptional efforts take place. One of the best ways is to empower employees to identify peers who have excelled. Employees are in the best position to see these efforts. Establish a simple, convenient way for employees to say, "Lisa Jones really did an incredible thing for a customer, and it's something all of us should consider doing." Once the exceptional efforts have been identified, it's up to the organization's leadership to recognize the people in a dignified, symbolic, and non-monetary manner.

- *Best practices to be adopted.* Success stories and recognition are nice, but if these successes languish in isolation, the organization misses a huge opportunity. Leadership should clearly state how the exceptional efforts of others could be adapted throughout the organization. Remember, leaders are supposed to lead. The direction they lead doesn't have to come from their own ideas. Best practices will come from a wide variety of personnel, and top management must be the first to institutionalize these best practices for the entire organization's benefit.

- *Where the organization has failed.* Smart organizations learn from their mistakes. Leadership should be honest and open about mistakes the organization has made and outline clear actions that will remove the causes of failure. Clearly, top management isn't going to personally communicate every single customer service mistake the organization has made. However, top management must explain critical mistakes. Doing so highlights the significance of the errors and captures everybody's attention.

- *Where customer expectations are moving.* Nothing in life is static. Customer expectations are continually evolving, sometimes in surprising directions. Do you know where they're headed? You certainly should, and top management should share the general direction with everyone. If the entire organization becomes familiar with where customer expectations are moving, they'll be better prepared to deliver on these expectations. Innovative ways to address new or altered expectations can come from all levels of the organization, but if no one knows about them, they can't be addressed.

Customer focus should be near the top of the agenda every time leadership communicates with the organization, and the communication can't be too frequent.

CUSTOMER FOCUS IS
LINKED TO EMPLOYEE FOCUS

I taught a course a few years ago at the Holiday Inn in Cartersville, Georgia. The hotel wasn't particularly special in terms of amenities, but the staff bent over backward to make our event a success. They did things I never would've thought about doing, including providing some supplies we'd forgotten. At every turn, I was amazed by the complete customer focus of everyone I encountered.

After the course was finished, I met with the hotel manager to find out his secret. How did he get all these people to focus so successfully on the customer? How did he achieve this miracle of managing?

"I focus on my employees," he told me. "That allows them to focus on the customer."

I hadn't noticed him standing around watching his employees. What kind of surveillance was he running?

"I'm not watching anybody," he explained. "I've never had to watch anybody in all the time I've been the manager here. All I do is focus on what my people need to do the job. I focus on their tools, training, and skills. I even get to know their families, interests, and personal problems. They understand that I care about them, but they also understand that their jobs are to serve the customer. The customer is number one, and my employees are a close second."

Just saying, "focus on your employees" doesn't provide much guidance. What should leaders do to focus on their employees, and thereby ensure a focus on customers? Here are the keys:

- *Provide the tools.* Leaders should find out firsthand what their employees require to do their jobs. Leaders should observe employees doing their jobs and think about what could make their jobs easier and more effective. They should discuss these resources with the employees and come to an agreement about their priority. Leaders shouldn't make any big promises, but they should make it clear that they intend to find a way to provide the resources.

■ *Develop the people.* It's a natural human trait to want to get better, smarter, and more skillful. Leaders take advantage of this trait and determine the specific competencies that will help their employees better serve the customer. They consider the full range of competency-building activities: training, education, skill-building, mentoring, role-playing, and new work experiences. Successful leaders make improving their employees a strategic initiative.

■ *Share information.* Another natural human trait is curiosity. For most people, curiosity is even stronger than the need for self-improvement. People want to know the reason why; they want to possess knowledge. The first step to possessing knowledge is receiving information. A leader should share as much information as is practically possible. Everyone is on the same team, right? If so, everyone needs abundant information about the direction and performance of the organization, especially in relation to satisfying customers.

■ *Take a real interest.* A leader's job isn't to get people to like him or her; it's to lead. Taking a real interest in your people facilitates leadership because you begin to understand what makes them tick. Is it fishing or chess? Is it singing or football? This knowledge helps you gain insights into their psyches, which enables you to better motivate your employees and communicate with them.

■ *Hire the right people.* Some people are simply more customer-oriented than others. A leader should always be on the lookout for people who like to take charge and make customer satisfaction their personal responsibility. Not everyone can be a customer service star, but all employees should be able to internalize the customer experience and strive to serve in the way they'd want to be served. Certain personality types should probably be avoided, especially for those jobs that come in direct or indirect contact with customers. These include people who are self-centered, grandiose, cynical, withdrawn, negative, angry, inwardly focused, and suspicious. It doesn't take a perceptive leader long to pick up on these attributes. It can be as simple as asking yourself, "Is this someone whom I'd want serving me?"

■ *Keep a sense of humor.* Leaders can't be serious all the time. They must be willing to laugh at themselves and the situations their organizations face. This makes the organization a more human and livable place, and it makes employees happier to be there. This in turn facilitates better customer service because miserable, humorless employees can think of nothing more than going home—certainly not satisfying customers.

Focusing on employees is the precursor to our next topic, which is enabling employees to take ownership for the customer experience.

LEADERS MUST DRIVE OWNERSHIP FOR THE CUSTOMER EXPERIENCE

Customer focus is too big of a job for one person, or even a group of people, in any organization. It should be everyone's job. Company leaders must understand that everyone in the organization must be empowered to drive customer loyalty. This means decentralized decision making, which can be a frightening concept to many managers. However, it's the only way to really achieve comprehensive customer focus. Top management must provide specific guidelines for what employees can do and when, and then let employees act on these guidelines. When customers have a problem, they don't want to hear, "I really can't help you right now, but you can talk to my manager in the morning." The morning is too late. The customer wants an answer *now.* Employees must have the authority, judgment, and training to manage customer issues that come up in real time. Only top management can make this happen. Standing up in a meeting and saying, "I want everyone to take care of our customers," is meaningless. Company leaders must define specific guidelines for what it means to "take care of our customers." This will involve documented policies that are shared with everyone and made a cornerstone of the organization's training process.

CUSTOMER FOCUS MUST BE
A TOP-LEVEL STRATEGY

Most of what's been discussed in this book so far has been outwardly focused and concerned with leaders shaping the actions of others within the organization. More important than these "shaping" exercises are what top management does about customer focus when the conference-room doors are closed. Are customer perceptions really used at the highest levels of the organization for decision making? Is customer focus really a top-level strategy?

Leaders must institute customer focus as one of the organization's driving strategies. The purpose isn't to motivate employees to keep customers on their minds, but to keep customers on the minds of top managers when they make key decisions. This can be accomplished in a number of ways:

- *Key measures that include customer satisfaction metrics.* Whether they're called key measures or something else, most organizations have a short list of critical metrics that indicate the organization's success or failure. Most of these measures are focused on financial results, and for good reason. Financial results clearly indicate how the organization has performed. The only problem is that they're lagging indicators, revealing what's already happened. Customer satisfaction metrics, on the other hand, are leading indicators, predicting what will happen. It's imperative that leaders include customer satisfaction metrics in their set of key measures. If they don't, they've missed one of the most important leading indicators available to the organization.

- *Analysis of customer satisfaction results at the highest levels.* Top management often reviews the organization's performance. For business organizations, this is typically done every month. Does this review include an analysis of customer satisfaction results? Do leaders even understand this is something they should review? Most of the business review meetings I've attended focused overwhelmingly on financial results. Customer satisfaction results were addressed by middle managers, if at all. The prominence of customer satisfaction must be raised dramatically so that it becomes an integral part of the organization's performance review, not just something that's covered if time is left at the end of the meeting.

■ *Heavy focus on trouble areas.* Customer complaints are serious threats to the organization. They signal the possible defection of existing customers and difficulty in obtaining new ones. Leaders must understand the serious nature of complaints and become personally involved in their resolution. Does that mean top managers must roll up their sleeves and troubleshoot processes? Maybe, maybe not. It does mean that they must at least recognize the current trends in customer complaints and decide whether they're being addressed effectively. In mature organizations, leaders are personally familiar with the top three customer complaints; that's how critical these indicators are to the organization's success. If top managers aren't familiar with the top complaints, they're neglecting their job of managing risk.

■ *Evaluating top management performance through customer satisfaction results.* A key indicator of top management's job performance should be customer satisfaction results. We've seen how customer satisfaction is a leading indicator that reveals the organization's future prospects, and top management's job is to build the organization's future. Unfortunately, few top managers are ever evaluated on this basis. Typically, they're evaluated on financial results, which does little to ensure future success. Making customer satisfaction a key evaluation criterion for top management will dramatically enhance the visibility of this measure.

To summarize, leaders must drive customer focus in everything they do. It can't be an afterthought or an extracurricular activity; it's a core job. When leaders understand and act on this, the organization stands a reasonable chance of evolving into a truly customer-focused enterprise. With regard to customer focus, leaders must:

■ Model customer focus in their day-to-day activities
■ Take responsibility for all customer-focus failures. All roads lead back to top management where customer satisfaction is concerned.
■ Make customer focus a regular topic of communication. Leaders should discuss customer service successes, failures, best practices, and changes in customer expectations. The more often these things are discussed, the more likely everyone will understand how critical a customer focus is.
■ Focus on their employees in meaningful ways. Employee focus leads to customer focus.

■ Make customer focus a real organizational strategy. This includes making customer satisfaction metrics a part of the organization's key measures, analyzing customer satisfaction results at the highest levels of the organization, and gaining a personal understanding of customer complaints.

■ Be evaluated on the basis of how well the organization satisfies its customers. This is a significant shift in the way top managers are assessed, but it's a policy the organization should strive to establish over time.

CHAPTER 3

The Process Matrix

All organizations are composed of processes. These perform the work of the organization, taking inputs (i.e., information, ideas, materials, people), transforming them in some manner, and producing outputs (i.e., goods, services, decisions, actions, designs). Ideally, processes are focused on the organization's customers, particularly their requirements and expectations. More often, though, processes are only superficially focused on customers. Some process owners might not even acknowledge they have customers. The seeds of organizational failure are sown at the process level when people begin to forget whom they serve. Processes gradually become machines that mindlessly churn out products, indifferent to the customers who consume them. For this reason, top management must work continually to reinforce an awareness of the customer at all levels of the organization.

CREATING A PROCESS ORIENTATION

Cultivating an understanding of customers at a process level is part of a larger philosophy called process orientation. This is an overall movement toward structuring an organization around its natural business processes, as opposed to functional departments that often create unnatural breaks in the true process flow. When the organization structures itself around processes, organizational members begin to see the synergies and interdependencies between disparate activities. Process orientation communicates to all employees how their actions affect others and how the entire organization fits together. Instead of functional areas working as virtually independent entities, employees respond as if they're playing on the same team with the same ultimate objectives.

Most organizations have fewer than twenty major processes. Many are linked, with the output of one becoming the input to another. These connections between processes should be considered as customer relationships. The organization should be as responsive to the perceptions of these internal customers as it is to external customers. Unfortunately, a competitive relationship often develops among internal customers. When the organization builds its process controls around the true needs of external and internal customers, and then takes action on feedback in a timely manner, competition begins to evolve toward cooperation.

A system of processes, all guided through appropriate controls and focused on customers, is true process orientation. The techniques that typically monitor and control processes are as varied as processes themselves:

- *Procedures.* These are instructions that guide people's activities. The best procedures are concise, focusing only on the parts of a job that require reinforcement. Troubleshooting and the answers to "what to do when these problems occur" are perfect topics for procedures. Brief checklists for critical tasks also make great instructions. Wordy dissertations make very poor procedures.

- *Photographs, pictures, and other graphics.* These visual tools can also serve as procedures. In fact, they're the best kind of procedures, easily interpreted at a glance. Graphic instructions are especially effective when posted directly at the workstation. Just like traditional text-based procedures, graphic instructions should focus on critical parts of the job. Some of the most effective graphics depict two conditions, side-by-side: the correct method (or conforming product) and the incorrect method (or nonconforming product). There's no mistaking this kind of simple and intuitive instruction.

- *Training.* Developing personnel through training is a fundamental process control. In many cases, training is all that's needed. Once personnel are trained, other controls are superfluous. On-the-job training is particularly effective when it's carefully planned and overseen.

- *Clearly defined responsibilities and authorities.* Simply letting employees know exactly what they're responsible for is a profound process control. So many problems happen as a result of people who claim: "I didn't realize that was my job." In general, people are very attentive to issues they have direct responsibility over. Communicate the responsibilities, provide authority, and back both of them up with the resources needed to be successful.

- *Automated monitoring.* Many processes can be monitored through automation. In other words, a computer or other machine oversees the process to ensure it's operating within the required parameters. This type of control is especially efficient and accurate. Remember that automated controls are often "dumb"—doing only what they're told to do and exercising little or no complex judgment.

- *Statistical process control.* When processes produce measurable outputs, it's possible to calculate the statistical limits the process is capable of meeting. This is an especially effective type of control because it's the process itself communicating what it can do. This is often different from what people think the process can do. When the statistical process control (often in the form of a control chart) shows the process deviating from its own capabilities, then operators know that something is affecting the process.

- *Work orders and travelers.* This is such a simple type of control that many people neglect it. Work orders, travelers, routers, and similar tools are simply documents that accompany the product or service through all steps of their realization process. They tell exactly what needs to happen to the product or service, when it needs to happen, and all other relevant requirements. The beauty of a work order or traveler is that it's mobile: It follows the same course as the goods or service, making it hard to overlook.

- *Measurable objectives.* Specific goals, against which progress can be measured, work almost like magic. They let everyone know what's important and why. When the goals are accompanied by practical examples of how people at all levels can contribute to them, you have one of the most powerful engines for success possible.

- *Records.* When a task is especially important, it's often matched with a record indicating the task was carried out. The record provides accountability and traceability to the task. Keep the records as lean and streamlined as possible, though, because it's all too easy to bury people in recordkeeping.

■ *Timely communications and feedback.* Establish regular methods of feedback between processes. Take every opportunity to discuss process performance and improvement, and be sure to include the customer (whether internal or external) in these dialogues. Every process owner should be able to point to at least one formal communication channel for receiving proactive feedback from his or her customers.

■ *Calibrated and capable measuring instruments.* Just like the products they create, processes must often be monitored using measuring instruments. However, there's no sense in using measuring instruments if they're not calibrated and capable of measuring with the resolution required.

BUILDING A CUSTOMER-FOCUSED QUALITY MANAGEMENT SYSTEM

Simply by virtue of existing, an organization has some kind of management system. Your organization's system might not be formal, documented, or complete, but it certainly exists. The trick is to take what you have and turn it into an integrated and cohesive system that drives overall objectives and facilitates customer focus.

Management systems, just like organizations, have a tendency to become self-serving and bureaucratic. That's why they must be kept lean and concise. The days of the giant binder of procedures are long gone. Develop elaborate controls and procedures only when the process really requires it. If a written procedure isn't really needed to be successful, then don't create one.

To be successful, smart organizations take an inventory of their processes, customers, and controls. They pull together all the fragmented pieces of the system and integrate it. As part of the inventory, they also clearly state who the customer of each process is. This inventory of processes, controls, and customers is called a process matrix. A sample process matrix is shown in figure 3.1. The point of a process matrix is to focus everyone on how the organization fits together and how everyone has a customer. Overly simple concepts? Maybe, but they're concepts that are too often neglected.

Here are the basic steps to developing a process matrix:

1. *Brainstorm processes.* Assemble a group of experienced individuals who have a broad understanding of how the organization works. Also include some newcomers to the organization to introduce fresh perspectives. With this group, brainstorm all the major processes that exist within the enterprise. Don't analyze the processes in this step; just record the output of brainstorming.

2. *Trim the list.* It's important to understand that some of the so-called "processes" that will be brainstormed are really activities. A good test is to check if the process is actually a set of simple tasks. If this is the case, then it's probably just an activity. Most organizations have no more than twenty major processes. The more streamlined and concise your list, the more benefit you'll get from process orientation.

3. *Begin the process matrix.* Refer to the example shown in figure 3.1 at the end of this chapter. The left-most column of the matrix shows processes you've identified. List all the processes in this column.

4. *Define the process owner(s).* The second column of the matrix identifies the process owner. This is simply the person or persons who have direct responsibility and authority for the process. Ideally, there would be only one process owner for each process. Because processes often cross departmental boundaries, there could be multiple departmental or functional managers who share responsibilities for a part of the process.

5. *Identify the primary activities.* This is where you list the primary activities that constitute the process. The list will help ensure that the controls over the process include all the key constituent parts. It also reinforces the definition of a process as a set of interrelated activities.

6. *List the inputs.* Every process has inputs that it uses to do its work. The inputs might come from other processes inside the organization or from external sources. Defining the inputs allows everyone to understand how the processes relate to one another, especially when the output of one process becomes the input of another. Depending on the nature and criticality of the input, the process owners may decide that the input must be verified prior to use.

7. *List the outputs.* Just as every process has inputs, it also has outputs. These represent the results of the transformation work at the heart of

the process. An output might take the form of a service, report, component, subassembly, final product, data, decisions, or anything else that's been produced. Outputs are the most obvious indicators of a process's effectiveness, and many organizations structure their monitoring activities around outputs.

8. *Identify the customer(s) for each process.* From a philosophical standpoint, this is the most important part of the process matrix. Every process has at least one customer. It's critical that the people working within each process have an understanding of who their customers are. As mentioned earlier, some people within organizations would deny they even have customers, which is a tragically flawed perspective. If a function has no customer, it's ripe for elimination. This point must be drilled home until it's embraced without any doubt. Remember that customers can be internal or external.

9. *Identify applicable documentation.* Most processes will have at least one document that guides their execution. The documentation can take many different forms: standard operating procedures, work instructions, flow diagrams, and process specs. Regardless of the type of documentation, the leaner and more streamlined it is, the more likely it is to be used. Smart organizations utilize simple visual documentation such as flow diagrams, photographs, and pictures whenever possible. Listing the documentation within the matrix makes it clear to everyone what document applies to each process. It can expose holes in the system and identify where the organization needs to direct its control efforts.

10. *Describe monitoring.* Every process is monitored in some way, sometimes in multiple ways. The monitoring may be qualitative in nature (such as auditing) or quantitative (such as measuring the number of errors). Monitoring is often applied to process outputs, but it can be applied at any other point in the process as well. Strive to make the process monitoring meaningful, not just something that's being done to satisfy a system requirement.

11. *Define the criteria for effectiveness.* What indicates whether the process is performing adequately? The criteria for effectiveness should provide unambiguous standards for evaluating the process. Ask yourself: What does the customer of this process care about? The answer will probably be your criteria for effectiveness.

The completed process matrix becomes the roadmap to the entire management system. It allows personnel to clearly understand how the organization's processes fit together, and how each process is managed. The matrix will also indicate where the management system is incomplete. The exercise can be used by any organization in any state of management system sophistication. It's especially helpful to organizations that are trying to renew their focus on customers, because this is an essential element of the matrix. It's also the element that requires the most communication once the matrix is completed.

Many organizations find it helpful to convert the matrix to a graphic flow diagram. This highlights the sequence and interaction of the processes and enables immediate understanding at a glance. Defining the sequence and interaction of processes is also an ISO 9001 requirement. The process matrix itself can satisfy this requirement, but the flow diagram supplements the matrix and provides a graphic check of the analysis leading to the process matrix.

Defining and managing processes through the use of a process matrix is the first step toward process orientation. True process orientation exists when an organization abandons functional-based departments and restructures itself around its business processes, each process serving a customer and reacting to its feedback. Organizations have traditionally divided themselves by activities. If a group of people were doing roughly the same job or working with the same kind of tools, a department was established. The only problem with this is that the activities included within this department may or may not constitute a process. Usually, the department was a subset of the true process. When departmental boundaries and process boundaries don't coincide, problems can occur. Every department attempts to maximize its own performance on the micro level, without really understanding how its activities affect the overall process. The activities encourage a competitive relationship with each other instead of a customer relationship. Because departments are essentially competing with one another, there's no incentive to share resources. Departments tend to horde what they need and operate on a semiautonomous basis, almost like a company within the company. This kind of mentality rarely helps the organization as a whole and certainly does nothing to drive a customer focus. In fact, this breakdown of customer focus, as small as it seems, is the beginning of the end of the organization as a competitive enterprise.

Smart organizations use their understanding of processes to begin a longer journey, one that leads them to redraw their organizational charts around their natural business processes instead of around outmoded groupings of activities. This is a journey that takes many months and sometimes years; sometimes it never happens at all. But the exercise of constructing the process matrix is a good start down that road. At the very least, it will heighten everyone's awareness of how the processes within the organization are related, how everyone serves a customer, and how everyone contributes to the organization's ultimate success.

To summarize, here are the benefits of understanding and managing the organization's processes:

■ *A more complete management system.* The process matrix provides a logical starting point for implementing any management system. It also indicates where holes exist within an existing management system.

■ *Clear identification of customers.* Every process is paired with its customer(s). It's easy to become complacent about your work when it's not clear who receives the output of your efforts. When all organizational members understand they have a customer and who this customer is, everybody's work begins to take on added significance.

■ *Broadened perspectives of all personnel.* Most people have a micro view of their organization. This is because they focus on their tasks and little else. Personnel rarely understand how their tasks and activities link to other activities, even when they're obviously related. A true process orientation fosters an understanding of how the activities link and interact with one another. Process knowledge creates a "big picture" understanding of how the organization works. A complete process matrix is the first step toward process knowledge.

■ *More efficient use of resources.* Processes by definition incorporate multiple activities. When we manage by processes, we're able to shift resources around from one activity to another. The competition for resources that exists when activities are managed in isolation begins to crumble. Why compete for resources when everyone is playing on the same team?

- *Smarter decision making.* In an organization that understands and manages its processes, decision making is based on what improves the entire organization and its customers instead of what improves isolated departments or activities. People understand how their outputs become inputs to other processes, and decisions are always made with the broader ramifications in mind.

- *Less need for supervision.* Because personnel understand how activities and processes interrelate, there's less need for close supervision. Personnel require supervision when they have a very narrow understanding of their actions. Process knowledge overcomes this obstacle.

- *Culture of teamwork.* An understanding of processes naturally reinforces teamwork because everyone can clearly see how the organization fits together into an integrated whole. The relationships between activities become obvious, and the walls that exist begin to crumble.

Figure 3.1: **Process Matrix**

Process	Process owner	Activities	Inputs
1. Business Planning	General manager	■ Risk analysis ■ Strategic planning	■ Environmental risks ■ Market research ■ Customer feedback ■ Organizational vision ■ Past experience
2. Market research and marketing	Director of sales	■ Explore new product opportunities ■ Set pricing ■ Develop marketing ■ Publish sales literature ■ Develop and use tools for capturing customer feedback ■ Provide advice for reacting to feedback	■ Market research ■ Innovation ■ Competitive data ■ Industry benchmarking ■ Customer perception tools
3. Design and development	Research and development manager	■ Understand market needs ■ Plan design activities ■ Review design progress ■ Verify and validate designs ■ Communicate design info ■ Maintain design documents	■ Design inputs ■ Creativity ■ Past designs
4. Order fulfillment	Director of sales	■ Provide product info ■ Provide quotes ■ Book and review orders ■ Communicate requirements	■ Sales literature ■ Pricing schedules ■ Customer needs
5. Inbound process	Logistics manager	■ Select suppliers ■ Communicate requirements ■ Place orders ■ Evaluate supplier performance ■ Verify incoming product ■ Ensure labeling ■ Warehousing ■ Material handling	■ Purchase order requisitions ■ Supplier references ■ Organizational needs
6. Product realization [*Note:* There might be multiple realization processes, depending on the diversity of activities involved]	Production manager	■ Schedule production ■ Perform on-the-job training ■ Produce product and/or service ■ Verify product ■ Calibrate all measuring equipment ■ Provide feedback	■ Customer orders ■ Delivery dates ■ Raw materials ■ Supplies ■ Electricity ■ Human resources ■ Tools and equipment ■ Product specifications ■ Engineering drawings
7. Control of nonconforming product	Production manager	■ Identify nonconforming products ■ Determine dispositions ■ Take corrective actions	■ Inspection criteria ■ Procedure for controlling nonconforming products

utputs	Customer(s)	Process documentation	Method of process monitoring	Criteria for effectiveness

Business plan
Key measures
Communication
plan for both
	■ The entire
	  organization
	■ Shareholders
		MGT-100-01	■ Internal audit
			■ Business review
			  meetings
				■ Achieving business plan
				■ Revenue growth
				■ Net income growth

Pricing
Design inputs
Marketing media
Trends in custom
er feedback
	■ Research and
	  development
	■ Sales force
	■ General manager
	■ Final customers
		MKT-100-01	■ Internal audit
			■ Business review
			  meetings
			■ Customer feedback
				■ Revenue growth
				■ Net income growth
				■ Results of customer
				  surveys

Engineering
drawings
Product
specifications
	■ Product realization
	■ Sales force
	■ Final customers
		MGT-100-02	■ Internal audit
			■ Business review
			  meetings
			■ Customer feedback
				■ Percent of revenue from
				  products less than one
				  year old
				■ Net income growth
				■ Results of customer
				  surveys

Customer orders Clearly defined requirements	■ Product realization ■ Final customers	CS-200-01	■ Internal audit ■ Weekly staff meeting ■ Customer feedback	■ Percent on-time delivery ■ Revenue growth ■ Net income growth ■ Results of customer surveys

Purchased
products
Damage-free
handling and
storage
	■ Product realization
	■ Final customers
		MGT-100-03	■ Internal audit
			■ Weekly staff meeting
			■ Business review
			  meetings
				■ Average unit cost by
				  commodity
				■ Percent on-time delivery
				■ Results of customer
				  surveys

Final product
Inspection data
Certificates of
analysis
	■ Outbound
	  processes
	■ Final customers
		PRD-200-01
		PRD-200-02
		PRD-200-03
		PRD-300-01
		PRD-300-02
		PRD-300-03
			■ Internal audit
			■ Line checks
			■ Product inspections
			■ Business review
			  meetings
			■ Customer feedback
				■ Percent of on-time
				  delivery
				■ Average unit cost by
				  product line
				■ Net income growth
				■ Results of customer
				  surveys

Dispositions
Corrective actions
	■ Product realization
	■ Outbound
	  processes
		PRD-200-04	■ Internal audit	■ Complete adherence to
				  procedure

(continues)

Figure 3.1: **Process Matrix** (continued)

Process	Process owner	Activities	Inputs
8. Outbound process	Logistics manager	■ Packaging ■ Labeling ■ Warehousing ■ Material handling ■ Schedule pickups ■ Shipping	■ Final product ■ Delivery dates ■ Packaging materials ■ Labels ■ Trucking services
9. Business review	General manager	■ Review implementation of business plan ■ Monitor progress on key measures ■ Analyze all other required inputs	■ Business plan ■ Performance data ■ Key measures ■ Analytical skill
10. Human resource process	Human resources manager	■ Determine competency requirements ■ Recruit ■ Determine human resource policies ■ Organizational communications ■ Mediate conflict ■ Ensure training ■ Ensure legal compliance	■ Organizational needs ■ Business plan ■ Personnel requisitions ■ Job descriptions
11. Maintenance process	Production manager	■ Develop production management schedules ■ Perform scheduled maintenance ■ React to breakdowns ■ Install new equipment	■ Manufacturer recommenda-tions ■ Predictive analysis ■ Skilled maintenance personnel ■ Supplies and materials ■ Spare parts
12. Internal auditing	Quality assurance manager	■ Schedule audits ■ Train auditors ■ Perform audits ■ Report results ■ Ensure corrective action	■ Past performance ■ Process criticality ■ Trained auditors ■ Top management leadership
13. Corrective and preventive action	Quality assurance manager	■ Perform training on problem solving ■ Administer corrective and preventive action database ■ Assign ownership ■ Track issues to completion ■ Verify effectiveness	■ Existing problems ■ Ideas ■ Potential problems ■ Trends ■ Data
14. Compliance management	Quality assurance manager	■ Determine legal issues ■ Analyze safety hazards ■ Analyze environmental impacts ■ Develop actions to minimize hazards and impacts	■ Laws ■ Regulations ■ Risks ■ Community concerns
15. Document and record control	Quality assurance manager	■ Ensure crisis management plan ■ Maintain regulatory compliance ■ Ensure availability of documents ■ Facilitate revision of documents ■ Dispose of obsolete documents ■ Maintain records	■ Process needs ■ Competency of personnel ■ Computer media ■ Degree of product complexity ■ Legal requirements

utputs	Customer(s)	Process documentation	Method of process monitoring	Criteria for effectiveness
Delivered product Damage-free handling and storage	■ Final customers	MGT-100-04	■ Internal audit ■ Business review meetings ■ Customer feedback	■ Percent of on-time delivery ■ Net income growth ■ Results of customer surveys
Preventive actions Business plan revisions Strategic decisions	■ The entire organization ■ Shareholders	MGT-100-05	■ Internal audit	■ Achieving business plan ■ Improving key measures
Trained personnel Legal compliance	■ The entire organization ■ General manager	MGT-100-06	■ Internal audit ■ Business review meeting	■ Employee retention rate ■ Net income growth
Timely repairs Preventive maintenance	■ Product realization ■ Inbound Processes ■ Outbound processes	PRD-200-05 PRD-200-06 PRD-200-07	■ Internal audit ■ Business review meetings	■ Hours of downtime per week ■ Net income growth
Corrective actions Positive practices Broad communication of results	■ The entire organization ■ Business review	MGT-100-07	■ Internal audit ■ Business review meetings	■ Net income growth ■ Improving key measures
Solutions Improvements Innovations Revised procedures	■ The entire organization ■ Business review ■ Business planning	MGT-100-08	■ Internal audit ■ Business review meetings	■ Complete adherence to procedure ■ Net income growth ■ Improving key measures
Preventive actions Legal compliance	■ Business review ■ Community ■ Shareholders ■ Regulatory agencies ■ The entire organization	ENV-100-01 SAF-100-01 EMG-100-01	■ Internal audit ■ Business review meetings	■ Amount of workers' compensation expenditures ■ No notices of violations ■ Complete adherence to emergency response plan
Procedures Policies Timely revisions Retrievable records Available instructions	■ The entire organization	MGT-100-09	■ Internal audit	■ Complete adherence with procedure

CHAPTER 4

Lean Processes and Customer Focus

Lean management means doing the most with what you have. It means cultivating efficiency and intelligence throughout the organization. In the modern economy, lean is a fact of life. Your organization's processes must be lean if you hope to survive. Unwieldy bureaucracies lead an organization to one unfortunate state: a lack of customer focus. When processes become complex and self-serving, the organization can't help but forget why it exists. The organization becomes inwardly focused instead of outwardly focused, and that's the beginning of the end for the enterprise.

Lean processes are easy to implement once they're understood, and they can make the difference between success and failure. Let's examine some fundamental lean processes for a customer-focused organization.

STRATEGIC PLANNING

The term "strategic planning" conjures images of grim-faced executives, conference tables cluttered with financial reports, and walls filled with scribbled flip chart pages. In other words, an intimidating and time-consuming process. However, strategic planning is critical to a customer-focused organization. It defines the organization's course over an extended timeframe, focusing all organizational members on the most critical actions necessary for achieving growth, survival, and customer loyalty. What the organization really needs is lean strategic planning: the essence of strategizing stripped down to its core.

Lean strategic planning can be performed in two to four hours. The underlying concerns are the same as the more time-consuming version, just with less philosophizing. Hot air and philosophizing add no value to the customer. Lean strategic planning will provide concrete answers to the following questions:

- What are we doing especially well? How do we thrill customers and surprise them with our foresight? What must happen to ensure we continue doing this effectively, and get even better?

- What are some of our most promising opportunities to better serve our customers or capture new ones? Why are they promising? What should we do to pursue these opportunities and turn them into things we do especially well?

- What are we bad at? What do our customers tell us we should improve upon? What do our employees tell us we should improve upon? Exactly what should we do to improve these aspects of our business?

- What competitors are threatening to take our customers? What makes them a real threat? What should we do to minimize the risks posed by these competitors? What other forces (e.g., social, demographic, political, economic, technological) threaten us? What should we do about these threats?

The answers to these questions are the heart of strategic planning. The answers will almost always involve taking action of some sort: changing a process, acquiring capital, improving an operation, or any number of other initiatives. The point is that strategic planning is dynamic and always leads to change within the organization. The things you want to change become objectives for the time period covered by strategic planning. Objectives are some of the most poorly understood tools in an organization, so let's see how they can be used more effectively.

OBJECTIVES

Even the best strategic plan can be difficult to understand for those not involved in the planning process. Objectives take the strategy and put it into language that everyone can understand and implement. They communicate an important message: "Here's what we think is important for our future success. Let's focus on these issues."

Although objectives serve as bright spotlights highlighting necessary action, their mere presence won't make anything happen. A good analogy is the farmer who purchases a bag of seeds in early spring. He might think to himself, "Soon I'll be eating corn," but there's a lot of work that must happen between buying the seeds and eating the corn. Your objectives are just like those seeds. They're a good start, but it will take a lot of effort to make them take root, grow, and produce positive results.

Once your organization sets objectives, it must reexamine its processes. If you want revenue to increase, then how do you expect this to happen? Through more aggressive marketing? More reliable products? Acquiring competitors? Just saying what you want to do isn't enough. You must have a plan to address the underlying processes. When you embrace objectives, change isn't far behind. If your way of operating doesn't change, then you're fooling yourself if you think you'll achieve your objectives.

Every objective must be matched to an improvement plan. The plan should address each of the following points:

- *Means.* You must state specifically how you're going to achieve your objectives. "Trying harder" isn't a good enough explanation. What processes will be changed? How will they be changed? What intermediate steps will be taken? Describe the means in a logical manner so they can be implemented.
- *Resources.* Change will require resources. The resources might include funds, time, people, facilities, equipment, and information. State the necessary resources, then make sure they're available before trying to implement the plan.
- *Responsibilities.* Who's responsible for each step of the plan? Clearly designate and communicate responsibilities, and then hold people accountable. Don't leave anything to chance.
- *Time frames.* The plans for improving objectives will take time to implement. How much time to do you think you'll need? Timeframes must be explicitly written into the plans, especially when multiple steps are linked dependently.
- *Contingencies.* Sometimes progress on a plan is contingent on other variables not directly related to the plan. Examples include competi-

tors' actions, suppliers, regulators, lawmakers, the community, and the economy, to name just a few. State the external issues that could possibly affect the success of the plan, then define what you'll do to help manage the contingencies.

Disciples of W. Edwards Deming are quick to reject the use of objectives in absolute terms. This is silly. Objectives are concise ways to communicate the variables of future success. When Deming demonized the philosophy of management by objectives, he was really criticizing the use of objectives without a plan to achieve them. Deming himself said quite eloquently, "Internal goals set in the management of a company, without a method, are a burlesque" (*Out of the Crisis,* The MIT Press, 2000). Of course you must have a method for achieving objectives, and the method must drive real change.

Strap on your seat belts when you establish objectives, and prepare yourself for a potentially wild ride. Your processes, procedures, methods, equipment, and overall philosophies could all change. You'll need a plan to drive and manage this change. Maintaining the status quo will guarantee failure.

Just like the strategic plan, objectives for each organizational process must be documented and made visible. A customer-focused organization must be a transparent organization. Progress against objectives should be tracked, posted, analyzed, and discussed. You don't have time to get fancy—just stick the charts up on the wall and update them regularly. The purpose is to provide a focus to everyone's work and to demonstrate how all activities fit together to achieve the organization's overall purpose of serving its customers.

BUSINESS REVIEW

Once objectives have been properly established, it's necessary to develop forums for reviewing progress. Customer-focused organizations don't have time for long, formal meetings. After all, when people are in meetings, day-to-day work isn't getting done and customers aren't being served. The work of the organization grinds to a halt. That's why business reviews must be performed in a brief, concentrated manner. They might not even be meetings. The review could take place over the telephone, via e-mail, through a folder of information passed from person to person, or by logging onto a Web site. The trick is to review progress and make decisions quickly and frequently because your organization exists in a dynamic world that's changing rapidly.

The agenda of a business review for a small organization can include a wide range of topics, but these are the most typical:

- Special or unusual customer orders or projects
- Customer feedback, including problems
- General communication between functions about current work
- Progress against objectives
- Improvement opportunities
- Generating action items to address problems or opportunities
- Status of pending action items

Additional agenda items can be added as needed, but remember that reaction time slows with each additional topic. Many organizations have found that their business reviews are most effective when they're composed of a number of different reviews, each addressing a different set of concerns. This "mixed" business review enables flexibility, timeliness, and fast response.

An example of a mixed review format—composed of a daily, monthly, and quarterly review—is shown below:

Daily review
- Requires thirty minutes or less
- Is tactical in nature
- Addresses the most pressing customer issues (e.g., urgent orders, necessary resources, or complaints)
- Is conducted at the start or end of a day
- Includes the status of pending actions
- Can be conducted in person or remotely

Monthly review

- Requires one hour to ninety minutes
- Is tactical and/or strategic in nature
- Reviews accumulated customer feedback
- Reviews progress toward objectives
- Reviews financial results (excerpted)
- Addresses the status of pending actions
- Includes broader trends (e.g., corrective and preventive actions, and audit results)
- Can be conducted in person or remotely

Quarterly review

- Requires one to three hours
- Is strategic in nature
- Reviews trends in customer feedback and actions taken to address them
- Reviews progress toward objectives and strategic plan
- Proposes necessary changes to strategy
- Analyzes financial results over a broader timeframe
- Addresses the status of pending actions
- Can be conducted in person or remotely

There are many different ways to slice and dice business reviews so they accommodate the unique requirements of a customer-focused organization. The only imperative is that they take place and that most of the review focuses on the organization's ability to meet the needs and expectations of its customers. You must keep a finger on the pulse of customer loyalty. That doesn't mean micro-management; it just means that everyone knows the direction in which the organization is moving and what changes must be made to stay on course. When these things are known, personnel are able to contribute effectively.

DOCUMENTATION

Documentation refers to the information used by the organization to run its business and satisfy its customers. The nature and scope of documentation will vary widely from organization to organization, but here are a few examples:

- Product specifications
- Service standards
- Process setups
- Procedures
- Job instructions
- Policies
- Engineering drawings
- Strategic plans
- Objectives

Documentation should be concise and presented in the most practical format possible. "Concise" means that the documentation addresses its topic succinctly and efficiently. More isn't better when it comes to documentation. Generally people resist examining information, so the documentation should get directly to its point and avoid peripheral information that's not really needed.

Practical formatting means that the documentation shouldn't resemble a traditional "procedure." Customer-focused organizations must get creative when developing documentation. Managers should ask themselves, "What format will deliver the information in the clearest and easiest way possible?" The answer might point to text, drawings, photos, cartoons, flow diagrams, physical samples, audio and/or video media, or anything else you can imagine. In general, people digest graphic forms of information more quickly than text forms, so including graphics is almost always a good idea. Whatever formats are chosen, the organization should try to steer clear of the following documentation paradigms that plague so many larger companies:

- *All documents must look exactly alike.* Why does this matter? Each document should look like whatever would best convey its information.

Consistency is only important if it adds to the documentation usability and effectiveness.

■ *Documents should always include certain sections.* The sections that organizations require within their documents run the gamut of possible topics. These include cover page, table of contents, introduction, purpose, scope, definitions, responsibilities, and reference documents. Although some of these sections might be relevant, others simply take up space and make the document longer and more confusing than it needs to be. Customer-focused organizations can't afford to make their documentation long and confusing.

■ *Documents must be reviewed and approved by every manager.* With good intentions, some organizations stipulate that all key managers must review and approve all documents. This only slows down the documentation system and adds useless bureaucracy. This subject is covered in more detail in the following section.

■ *Documents must include every single detail about a process.* The thinking goes this way: "If we're going to bother with documents, they're going to include every detail anyone could possibly ever need." The only problem with this thinking is that it makes the documents large and unwieldy, discouraging anyone from actually using them. Include the essential information, but strive to keep documents as lean as possible.

Anything that unnecessarily slows down the delivery of the information or complicates its understanding should be avoided. Get creative and don't be afraid to try something a little unusual. Some of the most unusual documentation styles are often the best for customer-focused organizations. Here are a few particularly user-friendly documentation formats:

■ *Flowchart and troubleshooting guide combo.* This is a single-page document, printed on both sides, posted directly at the workstation. It's often laminated or otherwise protected. One side of the document shows a flowchart of the process, describing the basic steps required to carry out the activities and make correct decisions. The opposite side describes various troubleshooting situations that might arise and what should be done about them. The troubleshooting situations utilize the collective knowledge and experience of everyone familiar with the process, becoming a one-page encyclopedia of the process and its pitfalls. The content of the document is limited because it's delivered on a single page, ensuring that only the most important details are included. The brevity also ensures that users aren't intimidated.

■ *One-minute reminder.* This is also a single-page document, posted directly at the workstation. It features a photograph of a particular aspect of the process, followed by a short description of what should be done, utilizing short and simple sentences. The text is often presented as a bulleted list. The intent is that the entire document can be digested in a matter of seconds, hence its name. One-minute reminders are developed at any stage of the process that's particularly prone to error or has a potentially large customer impact. Because these represent relatively few tasks in any process, this means that the documentation will be applied only where it's most needed.

■ *Hyperlinked process diagram.* This is an electronic document available on a shared drive or network. The document depicts a high-level view of the entire process, showing the major steps. Each step includes a hyperlink that drills down to a lower-level activity in the process. Document users can continue drilling down as low as they need to go into the process: process overview, activity-specific view, or task-specific view. The content of the document is completely dynamic, driven by the user's needs. Specifications for goods and services can also be hyperlinked from the main process diagram. This type of document is incredibly versatile but is only appropriate for organizations that have the computer infrastructure and technical competency to support it.

DOCUMENT CONTROL

Documentation is worthless if it's not controlled. Thankfully, the necessary controls are very basic. The fundamentals of document control include:

■ Approving documentation before it's made available
■ Making the documentation available where it's needed
■ Keeping the documentation up to date

Approving documents is a simple process. It's nothing more than making sure the information is accurate and appropriate for distribution, then making it clear that the document has been approved. One person can approve a document, and he or she doesn't have to be a manager. There are no rules about who can approve documents, except for any rules that the organization itself stipulates. Customer-focused organizations should keep the approval of documents as timely and streamlined as possible. There's rarely a need for a herd of managers to review and approve a document before it's put into use. I don't know how many times I've heard people say, "I'm not sure what happened to that document. I guess it's making the approval rounds." In the meantime, everyone is working against outdated information, and customers are liable to receive defective products or services.

Make documentation available where it's needed. Get the information out in front of everyone's eyes. If people using the information have computers, then electronic documents are often the best way to make documents available. If the users have workbenches, then hard copy documents posted directly at the workbench are probably more appropriate. Use good sense. Practices that don't make sense include:

- *Giant binders.* They're intimidating and confusing. Provide only the information that's needed.
- *Procedures stored in supervisor offices, training rooms, or other remote locations.* When documents aren't available at arm's length, they have little value. Put the information where it's needed.
- *Procedures provided electronically, but no training is provided on how to get to the documents.* I've seen this more times than I can count: impressive documentation systems that employees don't know how to access. If the method of document control involves new technology, make sure everyone knows how to use it.

Documentation is subject to change, of course. Customer-focused organizations must provide seamless methods for revising documentation. One out-of-date specification can make the difference between a good month and a disastrous month.

A decentralized document control system, with multiple employees who are in charge of their own documents, provides the most efficient process for revising them. When a document must be revised, whoever recognizes the need simply approaches the document control person in his or her process and initiates the change. The less bureaucracy, the better. Simply make the change, get it approved, and make it available. This is where electronic documentation really shines. Revising and approving an electronic document can be performed in a snap. Once the document has been approved, availability is accomplished instantaneously by uploading the document to the server or Web site. Everyone automatically has the most current version.

PLANNING AND FORECASTING

Work begins in most organizations by booking or forecasting orders. In a perfect world, business organizations wouldn't produce anything until there was confirmed demand for the good or service in question. After all, when organizations take a guess at future demands, they're often wrong. Being wrong means wasted resources. Too many wasted resources, and you're out of business.

One way to react in real time to demand is to maintain flexible capacity. This capacity might include the availability of equipment, machinery, supplies, personnel, information, or other resources. Ideally, an organization would always have the resources necessary for flexibility, but this isn't always the case. Few organizations have the luxury of maintaining idle resources just for the sake of being flexible.

A solution to the capacity dilemma is to establish partnerships with subcontractors that can help the organization react to demand in real time. Using subcontractors to carry out the organization's mission has significant risks. Subcontractors might not view your customer with the same importance that you do. The long-term significance of the customer might not register in their minds. Furthermore, the subcontractor's methods and procedures might be contrary to your own.

If subcontractors are used, the organization must develop the means for making 100-percent certain that they understand exactly what they must provide, how they must provide it, and any reporting or follow-up that's required. You don't have the time to micromanage subcontractors, but you must manage them. This can be accomplished by a subcontractor package that would include the following elements:

■ Lean, graphic instructions that guide how the subcontractor performs its work

■ Unambiguous customer requirements (e.g., specifications)

■ Internal service or manufacturing specifications, when applicable

■ A supply of blank comment cards or mini-surveys that will be given to the customer, in cases when the subcontractor deals directly with the customer

The more you can treat your subcontractor as a branch of your own organization, the better prepared the subcontractor will be to work as a partner and help you fulfill your mission. If you're suspicious that the subcontractor might steal your business, then you're using the wrong subcontractors. Noncompeting clauses in contracts with the subcontractor can also help reduce the chances of someone trying to become the primary supplier and cut you out of the loop.

The second approach for dealing with marketplace uncertainties is to improve the accuracy of forecasts. Many organizations have cyclical sales cycles. Some parts of the year are busy, and other parts are slow. In organizations that must operate in a cyclical environment, forecasts help dictate how and when to build inventory and capacity, and exactly what kind of inventory or capacity is needed. There's only one problem with forecasts: They're often wrong.

When forecasts are accurate, the organization can plan resources, build inventory, and manage for the future. So how can forecasts be made more accurate? The answer is remarkably simple: Get to know your customers. Really know them. Understand *their* customers, competitors, industry trends, core processes, suppliers (besides your own organization), strengths, and weaknesses. An intimate understanding of the business variables will help your organization paint a clearer picture of the future and what it can reasonably expect to do in terms of business.

Because not all customers operate in the same industry, it might be necessary to subdivide customers along industry or sector lines. An analysis of an organization's customer base generally reveals a handful of industry lines. For instance, a particular customer may serve the paper, chemicals, and pharmaceutical industries. The organization serving this customer would need to become familiar with the variables surrounding all of these industries.

Some possible lines of investigation might include:

■ Do you see your business with us changing during the next six months?

■ If so, what about it will change (e.g., quantity, product type, or requirements)?

■ How do you anticipate your business with other suppliers changing?

■ How do you expect your overall business to change during the next six months (e.g., increase or decrease in volume, new and/or changed products, change in product mix, or new customers)?

■ What are your competitors doing these days? How will their actions affect you?

■ Is your industry expanding or contracting?

■ What are the leading economic indicators for your industry? What direction are the leading indicators heading in?

■ Are there any new or emerging technologies that have the potential to affect your business?

■ Is there anything you'd like us to do differently to be a better partner? How might these changes affect our business with you?

Organizations that serve consumer markets can't subdivide its customer base by industry lines. They must study broader demographic and economic trends to develop meaningful forecasts. All of this sounds terribly complicated, but it's actually fairly simple. It just takes a little effort. The business faculty in local colleges and universities are usually willing to assist, as well. The typical methods of forecasting—to simply extrapolate previous trends into the future—must be abandoned in favor of forecasting based on real evidence. The evidence might not be perfect, but it will be better than forecasts based on hopes and prayers.

While talking to your customers about their business variables, make sure to tell them why you're interested in their affairs. It's so you can plan and forecast better, with the ultimate objective of serving them better. Few customers will argue with that kind of motivation.

CHAPTER 5

Fundamentals of Effective Customer Feedback

Customer feedback is the single most important type of communication an organization can receive. It's confirmation of the organization's purpose and its ability to deliver on this purpose. Feedback can ultimately determine whether the organization lives or dies. Despite the important and timely nature of customer feedback, organizations often treat it as an afterthought, something they might get around to if time allows. The processes for gathering and using feedback must be moved to the forefront of the organization's strategy. It's not optional.

What are the fundamentals of effective customer feedback? Let's take an inventory of the issues organizations should focus on as they develop and improve their feedback processes.

UNSOLICITED CUSTOMER FEEDBACK IS A GIFT

Every now and then, a customer will contact you unsolicited and let you know how he or she feels. I've even done it a time or two, usually when I was really angry or really ecstatic. In other words, I was highly motivated by my customer interaction. That's the trouble with unsolicited customer feedback: It requires a very motivated customer. Most customers have opinions if you ask them, but they're rarely motivated enough to contact you themselves to tell you their thoughts. They're too busy, too preoccupied, or don't feel it's their place to offer feedback. You must reach out to them and ask, "How are we doing?"

Organizations that rely solely on unsolicited customer feedback are fooling themselves. They think customers will reach out and provide feedback without being asked, but that happens once in a blue moon. Less than 5 percent of customers who have a strong opinion about your product will take the time and communicate their opinions on their own. This is the case for positive as well as negative opinions. You'll be in the dark unless you proactively solicit feedback.

Even when feedback is solicited, many customers still don't feel compelled to communicate their feedback. Think about the surveys, questionnaires, and comment cards you've received from suppliers. Have you ever thrown some of these in the trash without thinking twice about completing them? You might have done this because they were too long, too complicated, or too imposing. That's why your tools for capturing feedback must be as simple and streamlined as possible.

So, these are the first two imperatives related to customer feedback:

- You must reach out to the customer in a proactive manner and solicit feedback. Waiting for the customer to contact you is a fool's game.
- Your tools for capturing feedback must be simple and streamlined, or they'll be ignored.

CUSTOMER FEEDBACK
IS A LEADING INDICATOR

A leading indicator is a measure that tells us what will happen in the future. Customer feedback falls into this category because it reveals whether customers are likely to continue doing business with you in the weeks, months, and years ahead. Leading indicators are important because you can use them to gauge the direction of your enterprise and make critical decisions.

Leading indictors are relatively rare in business management. Most organizations use lagging indicators to gauge their direction. As their name implies, lagging indicators reveal what's already happened. Organizations are full of lagging indicators. Just think about typical accounting measures employed by businesses of all descriptions:

- *Revenue.* All organizations have revenue. Managers may refer to it as sales, donations, grants, or funding, but in the end they're talking about revenue. Revenue is one of the most fundamental organizational variables because it indicates whether the organization has funds to support its operations. The only problem is that revenue tells you what's already happened. If revenue goes down, then it's obvious that at least one of the following has happened: sales or support has dropped, competitors have made inroads, quality is suffering, or customers are dissatisfied. Revenue is an important measure, but it looks backward instead of forward.

- *Profit.* This is also a lagging indicator. Profit tells us how much money is left over at the end of the period after all costs and expenses have been tallied. In other words, it's the difference between inputs and outputs. Even nonprofits are interested in profit, because it indicates how well they're controlling their costs. Just like revenue, profit is a backward-looking measure. A drop in profit could indicate that costs have risen, revenues have dropped, unexpected problems have occurred, products are less valued by customers, or competitors are becoming more successful. Profit doesn't indicate much about the future, but it tells us plenty about the past.

There are countless other examples of lagging indicators. If you rely on them to help make decisions, then by definition you're using old information. You're basing future events on what happened in the past. It's important to remember history, but in business the past is no great indicator of the future. Just think of the many once-mighty organizations that have faded into obscurity: Eastern Airlines, Pan Am Airways, Braniff, and Montgomery Ward. Their past success would seem to indicate that they should still be thriving, but now they're gone. Their demise might have resulted from mismanagement, criminal activity, or a combination of both, but the consistent factor in all these examples is that the organizations weren't focused on their customers. The organizations were using lagging indicators to make decisions, instead of using the most important leading indicator available: customer feedback.

Few organizations include customer feedback as a key measure. This is partially a result of the perceived difficulty in capturing and understanding such data. It's also a result of top management not really comprehending how important feedback is. Sure, everyone gives customer feedback lip service and agrees that it's important, but it's rarely used for strategic decision making in the way lagging indicators are. Customer feedback is one of the few leading indicators in a vast ocean of lagging indicators. It's information that can tell you what will happen in the future. When an organization tries to understand customer feedback and bases its decisions on what it learns, then it's managing for the future. Basing decisions on lagging indicators is managing for the past, which guarantees failure.

CUSTOMER FEEDBACK
HAS A SHORT SHELF LIFE

Shelf life is a concept that people usually relate to food items, but it's also applicable to customer feedback. Feedback is nothing more than information, but it will go bad faster than a ripe peach. If you don't analyze and act on customer feedback quickly, its value will diminish to almost nothing within a matter of months. Use it or lose it, as the old cliché goes.

The reason for customer feedback's short shelf life is rooted in its nature. Feedback is based on perceptions, which are highly subjective. Perceptions can be derived from fact, fancy, fantasy, or fables, and often perceptions are comprised of all these things. People's understanding of their own perceptions can change or diminish easily. What someone perceives today may be different than what he or she perceives tomorrow. Because perceptions change so quickly, the value of reacting to perceptions also changes quickly. If your organization doesn't act on perceptions quickly after they're received, your customers will have already acted, usually by finding a different organization to fulfill their needs. Customer feedback is a valuable product that expires quickly after it's received.

The short shelf life of customer feedback is one of the best reasons for utilizing simple tools for capturing and analyzing perceptions. The more complex the tools, the more time will elapse before you take action. Some organizations spend so much time and effort capturing and analyzing feedback that they never take action.

Before implementing any process for capturing customer feedback, an organization must commit to acting on what it learns. The action must come quickly, too, if it's to have any real value. You may wait to take action, but your customers won't.

GATHERING FEEDBACK SHOULDN'T BE AN EVENT

Many organizations treat the process of gathering and analyzing customer feedback as an event. "We send out our survey once every two years," is a typical remark. Why make it a grand periodic happening, similar to putting on the Olympics? Doing this almost guarantees that the chore will be enormous, requiring a lot of time and money. A better approach would be to make the gathering of customer perceptions a continual process, something that's happening all the time in different ways throughout the organization. This enables quick action on feedback, which we've already seen is a key to success.

The notion of creating long, unwieldy customer surveys is very appealing to many organizations. The problem with this approach is that it requires capturing feedback to be a grand event. We've also seen how few customers have any desire to complete surveys of this sort, guaranteeing a low response rate. A low response rate combined with a huge outlay of effort equals a big waste of time. For so many reasons, it makes sense to make customer feedback something the organization chips away at all the time, a little here and a little there.

A wide range of people in the organization should be involved in gathering feedback. Mobilize everyone. If your tools are simple and concise (which you need to strive for), they can easily be administered by almost anyone. Relying on a core group of experts to completely administer the customer feedback process will work, but it's not the best way to approach the activity. The more people who are involved, the more people will understand the nature and importance of customer feedback.

TRENDS IN CUSTOMER FEEDBACK
SHOULDN'T BE KEPT SECRET

The grapevine within organizations is very effective. People hear what's going on even when formal communication doesn't carry the message. Because people are going to find out what's going on anyway, it makes sense to come right out and tell everyone. This is especially the case with customer feedback. There's nothing secret about customer feedback. After all, your employees are probably hearing informal feedback from your customers all the time. What they're probably not hearing and understanding are the trends in customer feedback. Employees are hearing part of the story but not getting the big picture.

Trends in customer feedback should become a regular part of the organization's communication. If you have a newsletter, trends in feedback should be regularly featured. Bulletin boards should include trends and specifics of feedback. Meetings of all types should include highlighted feedback. Any avenue of communication is a great place to share customer feedback. Don't be concerned that information on feedback will get into the wrong hands. People are going to hear bits and pieces of customer feedback whether you intend it or not, so smart organizations will package it in an understandable format and communicate it widely.

When employees are exposed to trends in customer feedback, they're better prepared to help improve their processes in a way that positively affects customers. The topic of customer satisfaction becomes engrained in everyone's mind. Communicating too much about customer feedback is almost impossible.

FOLLOW-THROUGH
ON FEEDBACK IS CRITICAL

Gathering and analyzing customer feedback is a critically important process. It takes a significant dedication of time and effort. However, if you don't follow up on feedback, the gathering and analyzing will have all been a waste. Follow-through is where organizations usually drop the ball.

There's nothing terribly sophisticated about acting on customer feedback. It simply takes discipline and a guiding process. Follow-through generally comprises these steps:

1. Analyzing trends in feedback
2. Identifying the most promising or most ominous opportunities
3. Assigning an owner to the improvement opportunity
4. Obtaining needed resources
5. Investigating the underlying issues and identifying causes
6. Determining action necessary to make improvements
7. Implementing actions
8. Evaluating effectiveness
9. Communicating improvements to customers

The final step, communicating improvements to customers, is critical. If customers don't realize that there's been an improvement, there's no improvement. Make sure to let your customers and the marketplace in general know the important improvements your organization has made.

To summarize, here are the fundamentals of effective customer feedback:

- You must reach out to your customers and ask how they're doing. Don't wait for customers to contact you.
- Keep your tools for capturing customer feedback as simple and streamlined as possible.
- Customer feedback is a leading indicator, unlike most other indicators that businesses use. That's why customer feedback is so important to an organization's success.
- The informational value of customer feedback doesn't last long. You have to take action on feedback within a relatively short time after it's received.
- Don't make capturing and analyzing customer feedback an event that only happens once every now and then. Utilize lean tools that can be applied all the time by a variety of people.
- Share the trends of customer feedback with the entire organization. The more people understand customer perceptions, the better prepared

they'll be to help improve them. Everybody in the organization has some ability to positively affect customer satisfaction.

- Follow-through on customer feedback is supremely important. If you don't take action—and follow through all the way to completion—then the process will have produced nothing.

CHAPTER 6

Developing a Customer Survey

T raditional customer surveys are ineffective tools for capturing customer perceptions, but unfortunately, they're the first tools that come to mind when people think about customer satisfaction measures. This chapter outlines the steps to constructing a simple and effective survey that will get the job done without driving you or your customers crazy.

There are many challenges to developing an effective survey. It's important to understand them up front so that appropriate attention can be given to them as the process moves forward. Here are the most notable obstacles:

■ Determining the key customer issues relevant to long-term success
■ Identifying survey statements that relate to the most important issues
■ Applying logical scaling to each statement
■ Including two or three open-ended questions to round out the tool
■ Adding instructions for completing and returning the survey
■ Constructing a streamlined and appealing survey package

These obstacles can be overcome by using a series of tools that guide the development of your survey. If you follow the instructions for each tool and apply some logic, you'll end up with a very effective survey.

STEP 1: ASSEMBLE THE RIGHT PLAYERS

When it comes to understanding your customers, nobody in your organization has all the right answers. In fact, the people who think they do are often the most inaccurate. That's the reason you need to assemble a small team of people (no more than eight) who represent a wide range of organizational concerns. Make sure to include representatives from production, quality, logistics, technical, sales, and customer service. Diversity is the key to success; it will help to challenge everyone's preconceptions about what's most important. Give all these people adequate notice that they'll be needed to assist in developing a customer satisfaction tool. Don't tell them they'll build a survey. Let everybody know the task will require two to three hours at most. There's nothing anybody needs to do to prepare.

STEP 2: DETERMINE THE MOST IMPORTANT ISSUES

Your team will begin by determining the customer issues that matter most. This is more difficult than it seems. Consider these three facts related to survey content:

■ An infinite number of issues could be explored through the survey.

■ Your customer has a finite amount of time and patience.

■ You must narrow the range of topics to those that have the largest impact.

The old paradigm of asking about everything under the sun is invalid. Your customers aren't going to complete a survey that takes more than a minute or two, so you've got to focus the topics. Unfortunately, organizations often don't know which issues are most important to their customers. Even worse, many organizations don't even know what's most important for their own success. Everybody enters the process with preconceived notions about what's important, but these perspectives can sometimes lead participants down the wrong path.

The customer concerns worksheet (shown in appendix B) will force everyone to examine the issues from a fresh perspective. Ask the survey team to break into subgroups of two or three people each to complete the worksheet. The purpose of this tool is to make participants examine customer issues from new angles and identify the few key variables that can affect customer satisfaction. Each section of the customer concerns worksheet addresses a different angle related to the customer experience. Section 7 summarizes the five most important customer issues bearing on the organization's success, based on the worksheet's methodology. Your survey should focus on the consensus list of issues from this section.

Here are specific instructions for using the customer concerns worksheet:

1. Divide the survey team into subgroups of two to three people each.
2. Each subgroup will fill out its copy of the worksheet, completing all sections.
3. When all team members have finished their worksheets, each subgroup will discuss its findings.
4. The survey team will decide on consensus answers for section 7, based on the combined work of the subgroups. Make sure the team ends up with no more than five selections, or the survey will grow long and unwieldy.

The team will now use the second tool, the customer themes worksheet (found in appendix C). The objective of this worksheet is to categorize the issues that arose from the customer concerns worksheet. The team should cross-reference the concerns in section 7 with the themes shown on the customer themes worksheet. If you can't find an exact match on the customer themes worksheet, find the closest match. For example, if one of the issues on the customer concerns worksheet is "problems with not being able to reach the sales representative," then the closest theme shown on the customer themes worksheet would be "accessibility." Determine a theme for each of the five issues that result from the customer concerns worksheet.

STEP 3: SELECT SURVEY STATEMENTS THAT MATCH THE MOST IMPORTANT ISSUES

Now it's time to match survey statements to the five customer issues that are most important to your long-term success. Appendix D provides a wide range of survey statements, categorized by theme. Simply go down the list of themes and select the most applicable, as dictated by the themes identified in step two. Remember that the sample survey statements in appendix D represent a wide range of possible themes. Some of them may have no relevance to your organization. Stay focused on the themes that were highlighted during step two and ignore the others.

All the statements shown in appendix D have the same response logic. In other words, an agreeing response is always good and a disagreeing response is always bad. The consistency is important because switching back and forth with response logic can confuse the respondent and produce poor results. As long as the statements are left as is, or altered only slightly, they'll maintain the same logic.

Depending on the timeframe within which the survey will be administered, the statements should be written either in present or past tense. In general, these guidelines apply:

■ *Present tense.* Surveys that cover performance during an extended period of time typically contain present-tense statements. Present tense has an inclusive, generalized tone that covers a broader timeframe. An example of this type of statement is, "The technicians are easy to contact." This statement is unspecific in time and thus covers all experiences within memory. If the survey will be applicable to all customer experiences during an extended period (say six months to a year or longer), then present-tense statements are appropriate.

■ *Past tense.* Surveys that cover performance in the recent or immediate past typically contain past-tense statements. When removed from a broader context, past tense implies action that's just taken place. An example is, "The technicians were easy to contact." This implies a discrete incident that has taken place recently. It's not generalized, but specific. Past-tense statements are useful when the survey will be administered shortly after the consumption of a good or service. These statements possess an immediacy that points to the most recent experience the customer had.

The survey statements in appendix D are all phrased in present tense. A little editing will easily convert them to past tense, if necessary. Get a colleague to check your editing if you're unsure about the tenses or grammar.

Finally, the statements in appendix D relating to people are almost all generic. They refer to "the employee" instead of a specific kind of employee. It's highly recommended that the word "employee" be substituted with the appropriate job title or role of the person in question. This provides a sharper level of specificity, which is always good on a survey.

What are some examples of more specific roles? Here are some of the most obvious:

Accountant	Doctor	Officer
Agent	Engineer	Operator
Analyst	Examiner	Planner
Auditor	Instructor	Representative
Clerk	Investigator	Scientist
Consultant	Mechanic	Specialist
Coordinator	Model	Teacher
Dispatcher	Nurse	Technician

For example, a survey statement related to mechanics would read, "Communication with mechanics is very clear," instead of, "Communication with employees is very clear." This narrows down the range of interpretations for the statement. The fewer ways a survey statement can be interpreted, the better. Unclear survey statements are one of the main reasons surveys are so challenging to administer and interpret.

At this point, you should have five survey statements matched to your key customer issues. The team should agree on each statement or at least be willing to compromise. Each of the five statements must now be matched with a response scale.

STEP 4: APPLY A RESPONSE SCALE
TO EACH QUESTION

Humans are unreliable as measuring instruments. We don't possess the accuracy or precision of a true gauge. The customers completing your survey are simply telling you what they think, sharing their subjective perceptions. The scale used for responding to your survey statements must be consistent with the nature of your measuring instruments, which are your customers. For this reason, a five-point scale, representing five degrees of agreeing or disagreeing, is the most resolution that can be reliably applied. Response scales with ten, fifteen, and twenty degrees of resolution are too broad. People don't have the ability to discriminate between such a wide range of responses, so keep the scale as simple as possible.

Appendix E shows three different response scales that are appropriate for any of the survey statements shown in appendix D. All the sample scales are agree/disagree scales, which mean they enable customers to say how much or how little they concur with each statement being made. Deciding which of the three scales to choose depends on your own tastes and beliefs. Choose one scale and stick to it. Don't use more than one type of agree/disagree scale, or you'll risk confusing the respondent and producing unreliable results.

Let's take a look at the three scales and discuss their attributes.

Scale 1

1	2	3	4	5
Strongly disagree	Disagree	Neither agree nor disagree	Agree	Strongly agree

Scale 1 is a five-point agree/disagree scale that includes a neutral middle point. This scale provides a reasonable balance between resolution and simplicity. The neutral middle point serves as the fulcrum for the scale, and the two points on either side of neutral represent equal intervals from the middle. The anchor points at both ends are equivalently opposite. The direction of the scale proceeds from the least agreeing to the most agreeing. There's nothing compulsory about this directional orientation; it could just as easily be reversed so the scale proceeds from most agreeing to least agreeing. The disagreeing-to-agreeing direction facilitates quantitative analysis of the data: Agreeing responses produce a higher score, which makes graphic analysis simpler and more intuitive. It's also worth noting that you don't necessarily have to include the corresponding point values related to each response. All that matters is that you know what the score for each response is.

Scale 2

1	2	3	4
Strongly disagree	Disagree	Agree	Strongly agree

Scale 2 is identical to scale 1, except it doesn't include a neutral middle point. Some people perceive a tendency of respondents to gravitate toward a neutral response, and they don't want to facilitate this rather ambiguous answer. In other words, they want to force an opinion one way or the other. The scale remains balanced around a phantom middle, but it doesn't allow the respondent to choose the middle.

Scale 3

1	2
No	Yes

Scale 3 only has two shades of resolution, yes or no. It's a study in absolutes. The organization either meets the criteria shown in the survey statements or it doesn't—it's that simple. A scale of this sort quickly identifies problems, because a "no" response requires no interpretation.

Scales like this are favored by organizations accustomed to viewing the world in black-and-white terms. Military organizations often fall into this category. They want to know if they met the requirements, and they don't see value in gradations of meeting requirements.

A yes/no scale is almost always paired with the request, "If no, please explain." This enables the customer to provide detail on the trouble area and provides the organization with some raw material for investigation and corrective action.

STEP 5: INCLUDE RELEVANT
OPEN-ENDED QUESTIONS

By design, we've limited the range of our survey to five statements. The statements represent your team's agreement of the most important customer issues, but they're by no means inclusive of all customer issues. In fact, it's possible that you failed to include an issue that customers feel strongly about. For this reason, it's useful to add a couple of open-ended questions at the end of the survey for customers to tell you whatever is on their minds.

The best open-ended questions provide basic direction to the respondent but allow for a wide range of responses. Many organizations find value in asking a pair of related questions: What do you think we do well, and what don't we do well? This solicits the good and the bad from the customers' perspective, and they're free to mention whatever is foremost on their minds. What customers choose to bring up is often something the organization didn't have on its radar screen. Open-ended questions can produce the most revealing and valuable information.

Here are some of the most typical open-ended questions:

- What's our biggest strength?
- What's our biggest weakness?
- What do you like most about working with us?
- What do you like least about working with us?
- What can we do to better to serve you?
- What can we do differently in the future?
- What else would you like to tell us?
- What can we do to provide world-class service to you?

Select two of these questions for your survey. They will appear after the five scaled statements.

STEP 6: ADD INSTRUCTIONS FOR COMPLETING
AND RETURNING THE SURVEY

Even the simplest surveys need instructions. These will appear at the top of the survey before any of the statements or questions, and they shouldn't comprise any more than a short paragraph.

Here are the most common issues addressed in the instructions:

■ *How to complete the survey.* This is usually related to whether the survey must be marked with pencil, pen, or completed electronically.

■ *How to save the survey.* If the survey is administered electronically, the respondent must often save the completed questionnaire using a unique name. Make these instructions simple and clear because people often have trouble saving files properly.

■ Where to send the completed survey

■ How to return or transmit the completed survey

■ Desired timeframe for completion

■ Whom to contact if the customer has any questions or problems

Here's a concise set of instructions that might appear at the top of a survey:

> Thank you in advance for participating in our survey. Please mark one response for each of the statements numbered one through five. Also complete questions six and seven if you have any other issues you'd like to tell us about. Please return the completed survey by October 1 in the postage-paid envelope provided. Don't hesitate to contact Craig Cochran at (800) 859-0968 if you have any questions or problems.

STEP 7: PUTTING IT ALL TOGETHER

You should now have the components of an effective survey. It's time to put them together in a comprehensive package. This is the sequence of elements for a typical short survey:
1. Title
2. Instructions
3. Scaled statements
4. Open-ended questions
5. Thanks and closing

Strive to fit these elements into the most concise package possible. They should fit onto one side of a single piece of paper or the equivalent of one. Keep the fancy graphics to a minimum; however, including your organization's logo is a good idea.

A couple of sample surveys are shown at the end of this chapter. Feel free to model yours after the examples, and take pains to keep your survey as lean and streamlined as possible.

STEP 8: IMPLEMENTING YOUR SURVEY

There are two general techniques for implementing a short survey of the type we've been discussing:
- Survey each time a product or service has been consumed
- Survey periodically, with the understanding that the survey covers performance over an extended timeframe.

The approach you take depends on the nature of your business and the relationship you have with your customers. Organizations that perform periodic services for customers often prefer to administer a survey each time the service is performed. This works well as long as customers aren't over-surveyed. Certainly, there's no sense in asking a customer to complete a survey more than once every couple of months; it will take at least that long for the organization to analyze and act on the previous survey. It's senseless to survey someone if you still haven't acted on feedback you've already received from that customer.

Organizations that have regular and repetitive business with customers typically find more value in surveying over a longer timeframe. But remember that the longer you wait to capture feedback, the less value it has. You're always trying to strike a balance between capturing timely information and not over-surveying. That's the reason that non-survey methods for capturing feedback sometimes produce better results. The best strategy is to combine your survey with other less formal methods of capturing feedback. The more tentacles your organization has in your customer base, the better and timelier information you'll receive.

Always remember the last (and most important) fundamental of customer feedback from chapter 5: Follow-through on feedback is critical. That means you must act. Capturing feedback and doing nothing with it is foolish and arrogant. Don't make that mistake. Prioritize the opportunities, make a plan, and execute it to completion.

Figure 6.1: **Repair Customer Survey**

Midsouth
Repair Service LLC

How would you like to help us serve you better? Your participation in this short repair survey will do that. Simply write your response in each of the blanks, and then return your survey in the postage-paid envelope. Please return it within two weeks. Contact Craig Cochran at 800-859-0968 if you have any questions or concerns.

Completed by: _____ Date completed: _____

Company name: _____ Location: _____

Date of repair:_____ Name of repair person(s)_____

1. Communication with the repair person was very clear.

Strongly disagree	Disagree	Agree	Strongly agree
1 ☐	2 ☐	3 ☐	4 ☐

2. The repair person was knowledgeable about the problems I faced.

Strongly disagree	Disagree	Agree	Strongly agree
1 ☐	2 ☐	3 ☐	4 ☐

3. The repair was effective in meeting my needs.

Strongly disagree	Disagree	Agree	Strongly agree
1 ☐	2 ☐	3 ☐	4 ☐

4. The repair person behaved professionally.

Strongly disagree	Disagree	Agree	Strongly agree
1 ☐	2 ☐	3 ☐	4 ☐

5. The repair represented good value for the money.

Strongly disagree	Disagree	Agree	Strongly agree
1 ☐	2 ☐	3 ☐	4 ☐

6. What did you like most about working with us? _____

_____

7. What is something we could do better in the future? _____

_____

Thank you for taking the time to complete this survey. We'll use your feedback to improve our repair services and become a better partner in your success.

Figure 6.2: **Post-Inspection Survey**

Please take a minute to complete this short survey about our recent inspection. Type your response in each of the fields, then save your survey using a unique name. Please return it to Craig Cochran at *craig.cochran@edi.gatech. edu* within one week.

Completed by: _____

Date completed: _____

Facility name: _____

Date of inspection:_____

Name of inspector (s): _____

1. I always understood what the inspector was saying.
     YES ☐   NO ☐
   If no, please explain: _____

2. The inspector was well trained.
     YES ☐   NO ☐
   If no, please explain: _____

3. The inspection took place in the desired timeframe.
     YES ☐   NO ☐
   If no, please explain: _____

4. The inspection focused on things that really matter to our success.
     YES ☐   NO ☐
   If no, please explain: _____

5. We'll use the inspection to become a more effective organization.
     YES ☐   NO ☐
   If no, please explain: _____

6. What suggestions do you have for improving the inspection process?____

_____

7. Is there anything else you'd like to say? _____

_____

Thank you for taking the time to complete this survey. We'll use your feedback to improve our services and provide you with a better inspection.

Figure 6.3: **Customer Survey**

Thanks for your continuing business! In order to improve our performance, we've developed this short survey. Please take a minute to complete it. You can fax the completed survey to (404) 894-1192, attention Craig Cochran, or e-mail the completed survey to *craig.cochran@edi.gatech.edu.*

Completed by: _____ Title: _____ Date completed: _____

Company name: _____

Address:_____

Primary products purchased: _____

1. Valves are always available when I need them.

Strongly disagree	Disagree	Neutral	Agree	Strongly agree
1 ☐	2 ☐	3 ☐	4 ☐	5 ☐

2. The valves are easy to maintain.

Strongly disagree	Disagree	Neutral	Agree	Strongly agree
1 ☐	2 ☐	3 ☐	4 ☐	5 ☐

3. I'm not concerned about wearing out these valves.

Strongly disagree	Disagree	Neutral	Agree	Strongly agree
1 ☐	2 ☐	3 ☐	4 ☐	5 ☐

4. Technical personnel are always interested in helping me.

Strongly disagree	Disagree	Neutral	Agree	Strongly agree
1 ☐	2 ☐	3 ☐	4 ☐	5 ☐

5. Valve tolerances are never exceeded.

Strongly disagree	Disagree	Neutral	Agree	Strongly agree
1 ☐	2 ☐	3 ☐	4 ☐	5 ☐

6. What's the best thing about doing business with Industrial Valve World-wide?_____

_____

7. What was the worse thing about doing business with Industrial Valve World-wide?_____

_____

8. Is there anything else you'd like to tell us? _____

_____

Thank you for taking the time to complete this survey.

CHAPTER 7

The Truth About
Customer Complaints

C omplaints are very misunderstood. Many organizations consider
them to be anything but what they really are: an urgent call to
action from a trusted source. When a customer complains, your
organization is at a crossroad, and one of two things may happen:

- You'll address the causes of the complaint, let the customer know the
actions you've taken, and strengthen the customer's loyalty to your organization.
- You'll fail to address the causes, never let the customer know anything,
and ultimately lose that customer.

A complaint is really a fork in the road, and the choice of paths couldn't
be more different. Go one way and ensure your long-term success, or go
the other way and strangle slowly on your own ineptitude. The strangula-
tion is so slow and gradual that people don't even realize it's happening.
Make no mistake: Ineffective handling of complaints can do irreparable
harm to your organization. Customers are giving you a golden opportunity
when they complain. It's a plea that must be answered quickly because the
opportunity won't come around again.

ONLY COMMITTED CUSTOMERS
BOTHER TO COMPLAIN

Why don't organizations recognize the critical opportunity offered by complaints? Because they don't see them as opportunities at all. They view complaints as distractions generated by people intent on being bothersome. Organizations fail to realize that only committed customers bother to complain. Here are some common misconceptions about complaints:

- *Customers complain only when they think we're not paying attention to them.* This view is rooted in the belief that not paying attention to customers is OK. Paying attention to customers is the organization's mission. If there's any chance you're not paying attention to them, your organization has a fundamental misunderstanding about why it exists.

- *Customers complain because they have nothing better to do.* This attitude indicates a deep disdain for the customer. People who hold this attitude believe the customer is nothing more than a carping pest, with no intent other than to stir up trouble. The reality is that complaining takes a great deal of time and trouble, and customers who do are sacrificing a lot to provide you with an important message.

- *Customers are just nitpicking.* This view stems from the belief that details don't matter. Details are everything. Customers who complain about details should receive special attention and thanks because they're delving deeper into your product than anyone else has. Far from nitpicking, they're performing an in-depth validation. Smart companies "nitpick" their own products long before they're ever launched.

- *Customers who complain are just trying to get a discount.* This mindset assumes customers to be penny-obsessed misers, which is almost laughable these days. If someone wants to save a few bucks, competition is such that he or she can easily cut the price he or she is paying. There will always be a lower-priced supplier. Customers who are trying to lower their costs just switch suppliers; they don't bother to complain. Why complain about something that doesn't matter? Customers who complain may be justified in receiving discounts, but that's rarely what motivates them to report problems.

The truth is that customers who complain are committed to your organization. This might sound strange, but remember that for a customer to complain, he or she must expend time, effort, and emotion. Someone not committed to your organization wouldn't bother complaining. The customer is frustrated by your inability to be as committed to the relationship as he or she is. The customer is so frustrated that he or she is willing to go to the trouble to tell you about it. Complaining customers are your organization's friends. They're partners in your success. Make it as easy as possible for these customers to provide you with their feedback.

SMART ORGANIZATIONS
MAKE IT EASY TO COMPLAIN

You must do everything you can to facilitate customer feedback, especially negative feedback. The nature of a complaint is so serious that all eyes and ears must be tuned to even the slightest hint of a complaint. Multiple capture methods must be employed. Think of your customers' convenience, not your own. My favorite customer-service snafu is when a toll-free number is provided for complaints and feedback, but when you call it you receive a message that says, "Our offices are now closed. Please call back between 8 A.M. and 5 P.M. Eastern Standard Time." Call back? Not likely. I won't call back or purchase this company's products again. This kind of message indicates incredible arrogance on the organization's part. It's as good as saying, "Tell us what you think, but only when it's convenient to us."

What should organizations do to capture complaints? Here are some options:

■ *Toll-free number answered by knowledgeable personnel.* Provide an easy way for customers to pick up a phone and call you from anywhere. Strive to staff the number twenty-four hours a day. If this isn't possible, provide clear instructions for leaving a message, and make sure to call the customer back in the morning. The personal contact is critical for telephone communication. People who choose to communicate with you by telephone usually do so because they wish to speak to a real person. That person should be knowledgeable about the product in question and ready to assist the customer. Wooden, scripted answers aren't welcome.

- When using a toll-free number to capture feedback, make sure to do the following:
  - ☐ Staff the telephones with knowledgeable people.
  - ☐ Don't give scripted answers.
  - ☐ Assist with real trouble-shooting steps (if applicable), but don't insult the customer's intelligence.
  - ☐ Capture all details of the problem if it isn't something that can be resolved over the phone.
  - ☐ Get the customer's contact information (e.g., phone, e-mail).
  - ☐ If you must use a recorded message during certain hours, provide a way for the customer to leave a message and make it clear that you'll call him or her back at the start of the next business day.
  - ☐ In all cases, let customers know that their problems will be investigated and someone will call them back with the results of the investigation and corrective action.

- *Internet Web site.* The Internet has become a huge part of life. Web pages, chat rooms, and e-mail are all commonplace tools. In fact, some people prefer these media to more traditional forms of communication. Organizations must recognize this reality and build their complaint-capture systems around their customers' preferences.

  Web-based complaint systems offer some distinct advantages:
  - ☐ Clearly defined information fields that ensure a comprehensive description of the customer's problem
  - ☐ Availability twenty-four hours a day, seven days a week
  - ☐ Accessibility from anywhere in the world
  - ☐ Consistency in the way complaints are captured
  - ☐ An impersonal approach that some customers prefer

  Along with these benefits come some drawbacks:
  - ☐ No opportunity to personally convey empathy about the customer's problem

- [ ] No ability to probe issues further, beyond the constraints of the Web tool
- [ ] Limited ability to provide troubleshooting guidance or quick fixes
- [ ] Impersonal approach that some customers find cold and aloof
- [ ] Perception that complaints may be going "down a black hole"

All of these drawbacks can be overcome by following-up with the customer by telephone or e-mail. The follow-up can be for the purpose of letting customers know you've received their message, soliciting more details, expressing empathy for their situation, or offering advice. The Web-based complaint system must have some interactivity. A one-way communication medium is unsatisfactory when a customer has experienced a problem. A combination of both telephone and Web site is probably the most effective process for allowing customers to voice their problems and concerns. Always remember that the complaint system must be convenient for your customers, not necessarily convenient for you.

TEAM PROBLEM SOLVING PRODUCES THE BEST RESULTS

Everyone enters a problem-solving situation with certain biases and prejudices. This is the case even with the most objective individuals. In a similar way, everyone applies his or her own unique skills and analytical abilities to the problem. It's rare that one person is objective enough and analytically powerful enough to solve complex problems alone. That's why team problem solving produces the best results.

A team of problem solvers draws from a wealth of strengths, experiences, and perspectives. The best corrective actions are typically the product of this kind of diversity. A team can moderate the natural tendency of individuals to jump to conclusions. After all, when someone is working in isolation, it's tempting to think, "Hey, I know the answer to this problem," before he or she has even examined the range of possible causes.

Organizations often leap into team problem solving without doing the preparation necessary to ensure its success, such as:

- *Defining a problem-solving method.* A problem-solving method is a step-by-step plan for how problems are addressed. Typical steps include clearly defining the problem, determining the causes, determining actions to remove the causes, implementing actions, and determining effectiveness. It's as simple as it sounds. However, you can't assume that everyone understands and abides by these steps. The method must be formally defined, communicated, and taught. Without this structure, the team dissolves into confusion and frustration. A problem-solving method enables everyone to understand how the team will proceed in the overall process. It also prevents people from short-circuiting the process by choosing solutions before the causes are fully understood.

- *Providing team facilitation.* Facilitation is key to managing team dynamics. Despite this fact, facilitation is often neglected due to time and cost considerations. I've often heard the remark, "Our people don't have facilitators when they do their normal jobs. Why would they need them when they meet together to solve problems?" That's exactly the problem: Problem solving isn't part of most people's jobs. It's something extra, and they might not be completely comfortable with the role. Team problem solving is an activity that lies outside the comfort zone of most individuals. A facilitator helps smooth people's concerns, moderates conflict, and enables the group to stay focused on the problem at hand. It's worth mentioning that effective facilitators typically don't shoulder the problem-solving responsibilities themselves. They help the team to work effectively on the problem, rather than actively participating in problem resolution. Provide facilitation, and you'll find the quality of your team's problem solving improves dramatically.

- *Applying project management to corrective actions.* Lack of follow-through is a disease in many organizations. Problem solvers get started with good intentions, make impressive progress, and then slowly fizzle out. The reason is that the first phase of problem solving offers a feeling of excitement. Few people can resist the challenge of investigating a problem, determining the causes, and brainstorming corrective actions. That's the easy part. The hard part begins after the team determines the corrective actions. There's rarely any excitement in implementing actions. It's hard work, sometimes even drudgery. Carrying out corrective actions requires discipline. You get this with simple project management. It doesn't have to be sophisticated. Project management includes clearly defined responsibilities for taking actions, accountability for results, reviewing progress at regular intervals, and an aggressive review to determine the effectiveness of actions. When corrective actions don't address the causes or are ineffective, they become more visible. That's really all project management is: visibility. The problem stays in the forefront of everyone's mind until it's 100-percent solved.

IF THE CUSTOMER ISN'T AWARE OF THE FIX, IT DOESN'T EXIST

Customers are rarely familiar with your organization's internal affairs. All they know is what they experience with your products. If customers have had a problem with a product, that experience is burned into their memories. They probably have no knowledge of the corrective action you've taken. All they know is the frustration and inconvenience they've experienced. If you've taken effective corrective action, you must let your customers know about it.

The final step of every corrective action on a complaint must be to notify your customers. Let them know exactly what you've done to address their concerns and how that action will benefit them. Smart organizations won't close a complaint until they've contacted the customer.

What exactly should an organization say to customers who've had a problem? Here are the specifics:

- *Sorry you had a problem.* This isn't conceding weakness. It's actually showing strength. The organization is expressing empathy for the inconvenience the customer has experienced.

- *Thanks for letting us know about it.* As we've already discussed, only committed customers bother to complain. They won't remain committed for long, but you have a small window of opportunity. The customer complaint is a rare gift. Only a fool wouldn't be thankful for receiving it.

- *Here's what we've done about the problem.* It's nice to say "sorry" and "thank you," but it's even more important to explain what you've done about the problem. Describe the corrective action in concise terms that anyone can understand. Make it clear that the actions taken address the true causes of the problem. The customer must be left with the message that you've done everything you can to keep the problem from happening again.

■ *We'd appreciate you giving us another chance.* The final part of the conversation is an appeal. You must directly ask for the customer's business. It's not something that can be taken for granted. In fact, there's a strong chance that the customer has already begun using the services of another organization. By reaching out to customers, you have the opportunity to let them know how much you value their business. You must ask for their business and let them know they'll be happy about the decision to remain a customer.

The objective is to leverage the complaint into long-term customer loyalty. This isn't manipulation; it's smart business and good human relations. Nobody likes problems, but customers like it when an organization makes an effort to address their needs. The organization does this when it aggressively attacks the causes of complaints. However, customers won't know it unless you tell them.

CUSTOMER COMPLAINTS ARE GREAT LEARNING OPPORTUNITIES

So the organization screwed up and a customer complained. OK, fix it. More important, make sure everyone has learned from it. Customer complaints and the actions applied to them form an important database of wisdom. There are few better sources of learning than complaints.

Customer complaints should be shared openly with employees at all levels of the company. They aren't shameful secrets. Discussing complaints is a value-added action in all staff or departmental meetings. The focus of the discussions must be on the processes and systems that failed to deliver, not on the people. "Blame-storming" sessions serve no constructive purpose. The specific discussion points are incredibly simple and require only a few minutes to cover:

■ *What the customer complained about.* Exactly what did the customer experience? This is often a revelation to people within the organization.

Focus on the complaint from the customer's point of view, instead of the organization's.

- *The cause(s) of the complaint.* The results of investigation into the complaint create some of the most interesting discussion. This is also where people learn how their processes have a direct effect on the customer experience.

- *Corrective action(s) taken.* The complaint is a lost opportunity if action isn't applied. The actions, of course, should address and remove the causes.

- *Why does any of this matter?* This is a rhetorical question that's useful for employees to answer themselves. The point is that the organization exists to serve the customer. If you're failing to serve the customer, then you're in serious danger.

The database used for tracking complaints shouldn't be a secret, either. This is a repository of wisdom that must be accessible to all. It's helpful if the entries are searchable by key words, such as "late," "billing," or "damage." When complaints arise, it can be illustrative to see if the same issues have come before and, if so, what was done about them. For most users, the database will be read-only, allowing people to view the entries but not change them.

It may sound scary to give employees access to the complaints database, but it shouldn't. Employees depend on the organization for their livelihoods, and the effectiveness of complaint handling has a huge effect on this. Employees have vested interests in helping the organization remove the causes of complaints. The more they understand about them, the more they'll be able to contribute toward eliminating them.

Some organizations have a bulletin board for displaying photographs, physical specimens, and action plans related to complaints. Usually it's posted in an accessible, high-traffic location, and it's updated frequently. It should feature not only complaints but also the positive things that customers tell the organization. A particularly clever board I saw was divided into two halves. The first half was green and titled "The Good." The second half was red and sported the title "The Bad and the Ugly." Customer praise was posted on the green side, and complaints and failures were posted on the red side. Both halves of the story were important sources of learning.

Because it was regularly updated and balanced in nature, employees were drawn to it. It became a rallying point for people interested in furthering their own and the organization's success.

To summarize, the organization must attack complaints as if its survival depends on their effective resolution. That's because the organization's survival *does* depend on effectively resolving complaints. A complaint is the final, fleeting opportunity to turn a negative into a positive. The organization can facilitate its success in dealing with complaints by embracing five core truths:

- Only committed customers bother to complain.
- Smart organizations make it easy to complain.
- Team problem solving produces the best results.
- If the customer isn't aware of the fix, it doesn't exist.
- Customer complaints are great learning opportunities.

USING CUSTOMER FEEDBACK EFFECTIVELY

Yokogawa Corporation of America is a leader in industrial automation and controls. Dale Griffin, the corporate quality assurance manager, shared some of his insights about customer feedback.

"Our experience has shown that customers who complain seem to prefer the Internet versus the telephone," says Griffin. "I suppose there's an element of human nature that prefers the anonymity of complaining from behind a keyboard, as it's less confrontational. This verifies the old adage that most customers who leave will never complain. They just don't want a confrontation. We also have a toll-free number staffed during business hours, with after-hours messaging and emergency paging.

"In 2000, we implemented a Web-based complaint system. A button on our main Web page allows customers to access the concern form. Submitted complaints are automatically fed into a Lotus Notes database. Quality assurance monitors customer submittals daily and assigns them internally for resolution. QA acknowledges all receipts from customers via e-mail, and a resolution is guaranteed. The database is structured with corrective action methodology built right into it.

"We also implemented a Web-based order satisfaction survey in 2002. The survey features five simple questions, each matched by a five-point response scale. An optional comments box is included to capture open-ended feedback, which often is more valuable than the scaled feedback. Negative comments and ratings of 'less than acceptable' are entered into the complaint system.

"Every shipment to customers goes out with a double-sided card that explains our complaint system and survey request." (See following page)

What has Yokogawa learned during the past few years about its customer feedback processes?

"First, I'd say that the toll-free phone number isn't used by our customers to complain," Griffin says. "Customers only call when they have a problem needing immediate resolution.

(continues)

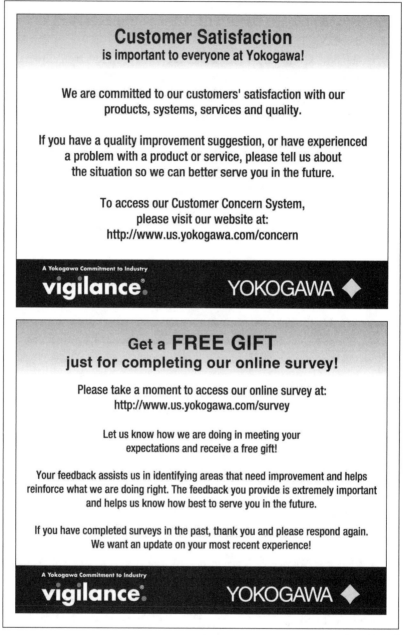

(continues)

"Second, we expected real complaints to be entered into our Web-based complaint system. What we got was something different, though. The inputs are typically minor and easily resolved (for example, 'Could you three-hole punch the instruction manuals?').

"The most dramatic thing we learned is that the comments field in the Web-based survey reaps a harvest of customer emotions. I'm not sure if it's due to the unstructured format or the immediacy related to the most recent order. It sure provides opportunities for improvement.

"Finally, resist the temptation to judge. It takes patience to understand complaints. In light of all that can go wrong in a typical day, hearing a complaint about the lack of hole-punching a manual requires you to stop, take a deep breath, and realize that what might seem trivial to you can be important to a particular customer."

Special thanks to Dale Griffin and Yokogawa Corporation of America. Learn more about Yokogawa at *www.yokogawa.com*.

CHAPTER 8

Training to
Drive Customer Focus

Training is profoundly strategic. It's a process aimed at improving the single most important resource in the organization: people. Nothing has more of an effect on customer loyalty than the behaviors and competencies of your people. Training is how you build these competencies.

Training should be straightforward: Figure out what knowledge and skills are required for personnel to effectively serve their customers, and take action to address gaps. The challenge comes in trying to build the system that will deliver on this. With good intentions, organizations often build unwieldy systems that are confusing and doomed to failure. That's why your training process must be carefully designed, with an eye for relevance, simplicity, and customer expectations.

IDENTIFYING COMPETENCY NEEDS

You must first understand the starting point for training, which is competence. Competent employees have the ability to apply what they know (i.e., knowledge) and what they can do (i.e., skills) in a job situation. It's a condition that enables someone to successfully drive customer loyalty.

The attributes that comprise competence can be categorized into four variables: education, training, skills, and experience. The mix of these four will differ depending on the type of job being analyzed. A college professor's competency needs would most likely concentrate around education and training, with relatively less emphasis on skills and experience. A glassblower's competency needs, on the other hand, would probably require much more skill and experience (see figure 8.1). Just as the college professor and glassblower have drastically different competency needs, most organizations will discover that they require a wide range of competencies, depending on the activities they perform and the customers they served.

Traditionally, organizations have built their training programs around so-called "production personnel." These are the front-line people who make the product or deliver the service. But remember: Everybody has the ability to affect customer loyalty on some level. Thus, the training program

Figure 8.1: **Differing Competency Requirements**

College professor's required competency	Glassblower's required competency
Education	
Ph.D. and post-doctoral studies	High school diploma preferred but not required
Training	
Formal training in field of research	No formal training required
Skills	
Ability to lecture and manage classroom	Demonstrated ability to produce complex glass assemblies, according to tight demensional specs
Experience	
Practical industry experience preferred but not required	Three years' experience working with a master glassblower, plus an additional two years

must encompass all roles within the organization and address competency requirements for all personnel. Here are some examples:

- *Top management.* This is the most neglected category of employee within the training process. Usually nobody is willing to acknowledge that top management might need a little training now and then. However, top management needs it more than anybody; its performance affects the organization more than any other function, so its skills and expertise require continual development.

  The competency requirements for top management can't be developed without its involvement and cooperation. This group must be actively involved in the process and made aware that competency gaps must be addressed. Competency requirements for top management typically focus on leadership skills, communication abilities, data analysis, and decision making. Instruction on top management's role in driving customer focus is also a necessity.

- *Professional personnel.* These are the front-office personnel who perform specialized tasks such as accounting, finance, human resources, and information technology. Many of them arrive at the organization with baseline levels of competency: college degrees, professional certifications, and previous experience doing similar tasks.

  Despite these qualifications, they must also meet forward-looking competency requirements. These usually relate to further developing their skills in their areas of specialty, broadening of their expertise across other functions, and understanding core business processes that might elude them on a day-to-day basis.

- *Production personnel.* Most organizations do a decent job of determining competency requirements for their production personnel. This success is driven by necessity. If production personnel aren't competent, then the product will be defective and customers will be negatively affected. Competency requirements of production personnel typically focus on training and skills directly related to their production activities (e.g., how to run equipment, access instructions and specifications, communicate with customers, and minimize safety hazards). Smart organizations will also include competencies such as using problem-solving tools, cross-training in different functions, and process troubleshooting.

- *Supervisors.* Supervisors get results by guiding and motivating other personnel, and by enforcing organizational policy on a tactical level. Supervision is one of life's most challenging endeavors. Many are called to supervise, but few do it effectively. Competency requirements for supervisors often focus on basic interpersonal and managerial skills. Continual training on labor laws, organizational policy, conflict mediation, meeting facilitation, and problem solving are also addressed.

- *Temporary employees.* Temps are attractive to many organizations, for a simple reason: flexibility. Temporary employees enable an organization to react quickly to opportunities and control costs. But temps are often ignored within the training process because the effort isn't perceived as a good value. After all, they're only temporary, right? However, temps carry out critical tasks and have just as many chances to make mistakes and hamper customer satisfaction as anybody else.

  Competency requirements are often very streamlined and focused directly at the task to be performed. Such a bare-bones approach makes sense for many organizations using temporary personnel. What doesn't make sense is completely ignoring their competency requirements.

- *Research and technical personnel.* The competency requirements for this category of personnel changes as often as the technology underlying their jobs. Determining competency becomes almost a moving target because of the highly volatile nature of the field in which these people work. In fact, competency requirements for technical personnel are typically established on an individual basis and revised annually, sometimes more often.

- *Recent hires.* Recent hires come into the organization knowing little about its guiding principles, values, and strategies. On a more basic level, they probably don't know the organization's products, customers, processes, size, and history. Orientation training on all these topics helps to put the organization in a meaningful context and paves the way for more specific training related to the tasks the employee will carry out. Orientation training also covers items of a personal interest to employees such as employment policies, benefits, and pay cycles.

- *All personnel.* Certain kinds of competency requirements are applicable to all personnel. These include the organization's mission, measurable objectives, customers, safety concerns, and basic emergency procedures.

Many personnel can be grouped together based on common roles and job functions. Just because two employees have different job titles doesn't mean they have different competency requirements. The converse is also true. Personnel working in the same area and ostensibly doing the same job could have differing competency requirements. Organizations must break down existing paradigms regarding the way work is performed and who performs it. Thinking about the organization as a series of processes that have different levels of customers (both internal and external) is helpful. When performed thoughtfully, determining competency requirements is often an eye-opening exercise.

Competency requirements should meet the following criteria to be fully effective and useful:

■ *Realistic.* Competency requirements must reflect the true needs of the activity being performed. Job descriptions, dog-eared and handed down through the years, probably won't provide any guidance whatsoever. Go out and watch the job being performed, then talk to the person doing the job as well as to his or her supervisor. Get input from the customers (internal and external) who receive the output of the job. Nobody is better prepared to provide competency requirements than the customer. And don't overstate competency needs; make sure a job really requires a college degree and two years' experience before stating these qualifications as essential.

■ *Demonstrable.* Particularly as they relate to skills, competency needs should be demonstrable by the person performing the activity. This means the organization must be specific and descriptive when defining competency. "Good work habits" is vague; break it down into its demonstrable elements (e.g., "ability to prepare written reports, use computer word processing programs, and deliver formal presentations to top management"). When competency needs are clearly defined, it will be much easier to identify gaps.

■ *Documented.* Documentation is the tool that codifies competency requirements for all to understand. Without documentation, how will the organization ensure consistent application and communication of competencies? Keep the documentation lean and simple.

- *Forward-looking.* The organization should consider present as well as future needs to the extent they can be predicted. Consider where customer expectations are moving in the future. This is where training and strategy begin to intersect. Remember that the forward-looking view of competency must still be based in reality. Competency needs probably can't look more than a few years into the future and still remain realistic.

COST-EFFECTIVE TRAINING

Once competency needs have been determined for the full range of personnel who perform work that affects quality, the organization must compare individuals to the competency needs for their functions and identify where gaps exist. Training and other actions are then applied based on the gaps in competency. This approach can result in significant cost savings because the organization provides training only where it's needed. It also sends a valuable signal to employees that the organization understands the needs of a given job or function and is willing to ensure that employees possess the education, training, skills, and experience to succeed in that role.

A wide range of actions can satisfy gaps in competency, and the overall process might include a combination of options. Examples include:

- On-the-job training
- Classroom training
- Self-study (e.g., traditional, audio, video, and Internet-based)
- Degree and certificate programs through colleges and universities
- Coaching and counseling
- Seminars and conferences
- Apprenticeship programs
- Mentors or role models
- Transfer to other jobs to gain experience

Obviously, training should be applied in as timely a manner as possible after the competency gaps have been identified. Allowing a significant amount of time to pass will only diminish the actions' relevance. Remember that training is a complex undertaking and shouldn't be attempted on an ad-hoc basis. Just like everything else in the management system, training must be carefully planned. Even on-the-job training must be planned and carried out in a controlled manner. In fact, on-the-job training usually requires even more planning because of the range of variables that interact in the job environment. The planning should specify timeframes, expectations, and measures. Once the planning has been carried out, the details should be communicated to the person slated to receive the training. Proactive communication will include answers to the following questions:

- How long will the training last?
- Should I do anything prior to the training to prepare?
- Where's the training, and how do I get there?
- What are the start and finish times?
- Will breaks and meals be provided?
- Are overnight accommodations necessary? If so, how do I make arrangements?
- What sorts of materials or tools will I need to bring, if any?
- In the event of an emergency, how can someone reach me?
- Are there multiple phases to the training and, if so, what are they?
- Will there be a test? If the answer is yes, then a whole new range of questions becomes relevant. Test-taking is a traumatic experience for many adult learners. Some typical questions include: When will the test take place? How will I prepare for the test? How long will I have to take it? When will I know the results? What happens if I fail?
- And, finally, what are the ultimate objectives of the training?

The person who receives the training should have a clear understanding of why he or she is doing it and how it relates to his or her competency. If effective communication has taken place, nobody will ever be heard saying, "They sent me to this training, but darned if I know why!" Communication should also portray training as a twofold opportunity: 1) to increase skills and knowledge, and possibly broaden career options; and 2) to invest in one of the organization's most important resources and directly affect its customers. If presented and delivered in this way, training becomes the epitome of the "win-win" relationship. Training should never be portrayed as punitive unless the organization is fond of wasting its money. Punishment in any form, even training, is rarely received willingly.

Awareness training on the importance of employees' activities in serving customers is also important. Each person must understand how he or she contributes to reaching the organization's objectives. This is more complex than it sounds. When correctly applied, awareness training will have three results: Employees will fully understand their customers, they'll clearly understand the organization's objectives, and they'll understand how their actions—whether packing boxes, driving a forklift, or processing contracts—contribute every day toward driving customer loyalty and achieving the organization's strategic objectives. These are among the most powerful concepts an organization can provide training on.

EVALUATING EFFECTIVENESS

Once training has been completed, the organization must evaluate the effectiveness of the actions taken. The best method for doing this is through customer feedback. Whether the customers are internal or external, their perceptions are the best indicators of whether training achieved the desired effect. An evaluation of training effectiveness can be included in customer surveys and other tools.

Organizations sometimes bristle at the idea of asking their customers if they believe that organizational members have received effective training. Remember: The customer is the bottom line. It doesn't matter if an employee has received years of training; if the customer doesn't perceive effective training, then you have a problem.

Another forum for evaluating training effectiveness is the periodic performance review. Most organizations already have existing performance reviews of some sort. As long as a logical connection can be made between the training and the job performance, the system will work. One important word of caution, however: Make sure to separate the performance review record from the training effectiveness evaluation record.

Many other methods can also be used for evaluating the effectiveness of training. These include inspecting an employee's work or product. For employees who produce a tangible good or deliver a service, this is often a reasonable indicator of whether training has had the desired effect. Many organizations already have existing systems for inspecting their products, and these can be channeled into the training program. However, this will work only if the product's inspection is traceable back to individual employees.

Tests can be used to evaluate training effectiveness, too. Be aware that many individuals simply don't perform well on formal tests, regardless of the quality of the instruction and training materials, so this might not be an ideal gauge. Another drawback is that tests require extensive administration: creating the tests, ensuring that all learning objectives are addressed, creating answer keys, creating a grading scale, taking time to grade the tests, and dealing with test anxiety and disappointment. Tests do have the advantage of providing a numerical score, which is easy to quantify and track over time.

Finally, it's possible for the trainees to simply rate the effectiveness of the training themselves. Clearly, this won't provide the most objective evaluation, but objectivity isn't necessary unless the organization makes it a requirement. For certain kinds of training, such as attending seminars and conferences, having the trainee rate the effectiveness might be a practical and user-friendly approach.

RECORD KEEPING

Record keeping is the last major issue to consider within the training program. The fewer individual records, the better—particularly if they're kept on paper. Electronic training records present a huge opportunity for many organizations. They clearly and quickly show what training has taken place, or is due to take place, and the gaps in training are obvious. Anyone who has been through an audit of paper training records will understand the pitfalls of the paper approach. Relational databases (such as dBase and Microsoft Access) and even spreadsheets (such as Lotus 1-2-3, Microsoft Excel, and Corel Quattro Pro) can be used to maintain training

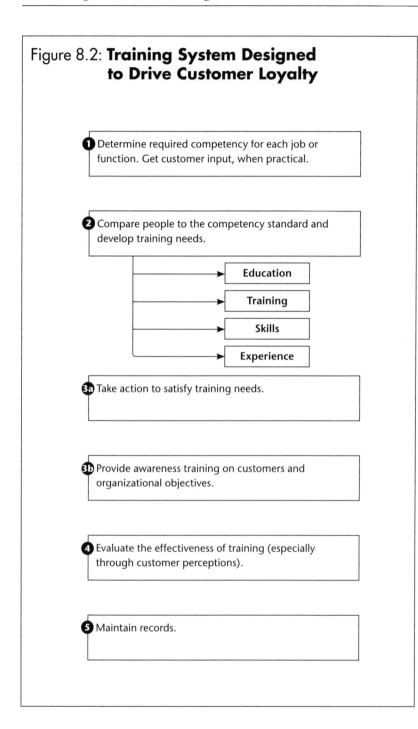

Figure 8.2: **Training System Designed to Drive Customer Loyalty**

records, and a standard PC is the only hardware required. The long-term costs of administering electronic records are usually less than the costs of administering paper records, as well. Make sure to maintain appropriate backup of electronic files.

Figure 8.2 depicts an integrated training system based on competency. The benefits of competence-based training are many: focused training that addresses the individual needs of personnel, lower overall costs (training is provided only where needed), more effective training, and a better understanding of the jobs and activities being performed within the organization. The additional planning required to implement such a system will easily be offset by the benefits, and the end result will be an improvement of the organization's overall performance through a better trained and more competent workforce.

THE TOP TEN TRAINING TOPICS FOR CUSTOMER LOYALTY

As stated earlier, employee training has a more immediate effect on customer loyalty than just about any other issue. The trick is deciding what the training should address. There are countless topics on which employees can be trained, but training resources are finite. Organizations must choose the critical few training topics that drive customer focus and the organization's long-term success. What are these topics? Here are ten of the most critical:

■ *The organization's mission and strategy.* The mission is an organization's core reason for existence. We've already decided that the core reason for an organization's existence is serving its customers. Employees must understand this fact in no uncertain terms. The message should come from the highest levels of the organization to reinforce its credibility.

Strategy defines exactly how the organization is going to deliver on its mission. Many organizations treat their strategies as big secrets. The problem with secrets is that they aren't good communication tools. If employees are going to help drive the organization's strategy (which they must for it to work), then they have to understand exactly what the strategy is. Pick the relevant pieces of the strategy that relate

to individuals' roles as customer-service specialists within the organization. When the strategy clearly focuses on customers and their
expectations, its relevance becomes obvious to everyone.

■ *How to present a professional appearance and attitude.* Professionalism is
an attribute that has become increasingly rare. How many times have
you been disgusted by the appearance and attitude of someone who is
supposed to be serving you? It's an almost daily occurrence. Disgusting
and disinterested employees are among the biggest liabilities an organization can possess.

The best way to let employees understand how they should look
and act is to provide explicit guidelines. Don't leave it up to individuals'
powers of creativity and interpretation; give them clear rules for dress
and behavior. Then enforce the rules consistently for all organizational
members.

■ *Handling customer complaints.* Even in the best organizations, customers sometimes complain. But this fact isn't nearly as important as how
the organization deals with the complaints. All employees who have
even a remote chance of receiving a customer complaint should receive
training on how to record the complaint, what kind of details to capture, where the complaint should go after being recorded, and how to
empathize with the customer in an appropriate manner. Nothing irri-
tates customers as much as employees who don't know how to handle
complaints. This kind of ignorance only makes a bad situation much
worse. On the other hand, employees who are trained in handling complaints can diffuse potential disasters and build customer loyalty.

■ *Effective communication.* Communication is one of the weakest competencies within organizations. It's also a weakness that has an enormous
effect on customer loyalty and satisfaction. When employees can't communicate clearly, problems are bound to happen: customer requirements are lost, messages are muddled, information is misinterpreted,
and people inevitably get angry. It's categorically impossible to breed
customer loyalty when employees can't communicate effectively.

Employees should receive training on the types of communication
most appropriate to their customer interactions. These include:

☐ *Listening skills.* This is possibly the weakest link in the communication formula. Simply put, most people like to talk but few like to

listen. Organizational members must understand that listening to customers, and really understanding what they're saying, is absolutely critical.

☐ *Nonverbal communication.* The way somebody stands, sits, and moves often conveys much more than words. Training should include guidance on appropriate nonverbal communication.

☐ *Proper use of language.* English is a constantly evolving language. Despite this fact, there should still be very clear guidelines for how employees speak and the kind of words they use. Language to be avoided at all costs includes slang, street rap, profanity, off-color humor, derogatory remarks, and political rants.

☐ *Written communication.* As difficult as verbal and nonverbal communication is, written communication is even more difficult. One of the reasons for this is that written words are often misinterpreted. Written communication must be carefully constructed, with an eye toward simplicity and brevity. Employees must get plenty of opportunities to practice writing skills, along with feedback on the effectiveness of their writing.

■ *Time management.* Failure to manage time means that customers won't be served. This fact is unavoidable. Despite this certainty, organizations rarely provide guidance on how employees can best use their time. Instead, organizations tend to build bureaucracies that ensure employees will fail to use their time effectively. Some of the keys to time management include planning each day in advance, prioritizing tasks, avoiding activities that distract from priorities, conducting meetings that are brief and timely, and providing information at the point of use. Removing nonwork-related temptations, such as unlimited Internet surfing and chatting with friends on the telephone, also assists with time management. A little bit of oversight usually goes a long way.

■ *Root cause analysis.* The ability to investigate a problem and identify its root cause is critical to customer loyalty. After all, most customers are willing to endure occasional problems if the organization aggressively attacks the causes of the problems and prevents recurrence. Inability to address the root cause guarantees customer defections.

Everyone in the organization should receive training on problem solving, root cause analysis, and using simple analytical tools. You don't need an expensive Six Sigma program, just basic tools that enable everyone to contribute to problem resolution. After receiving training, employees need the opportunity to practice. Effective root cause analysis is a skill that rarely comes naturally.

■ *Safety.* Why should customers care if your employees are safe? Because a lack of safety delays processes, causes defects, and drives up costs. Ultimately, a lack of safety will doom the organization. Training employees to work in a safe manner might not ensure customer loyalty, but a lack of safety will certainly affect it negatively over the long term.

■ *Business ethics.* Remember all those fundamentals that everyone learned in kindergarten? Don't lie, don't cheat, don't steal, play nice. These principles can be lumped into a category called business ethics. During the last couple of decades, the notion of ethics has seemed quaint and outmoded to some organizations. Their attitude seems to be, "We're here to succeed, and we're going to do anything it takes to be No. 1." Never mind if that results in unethical and sometimes illegal behavior.

Unethical behavior can destroy an organization. Reputable customers don't want to associate with organizations that bend rules and violate accepted standards of conduct. Employee training should include specific guidelines on ethical practices, with a lot of examples that people can relate to. Then it's up to top management to model ethical behavior in its day-to-day activities. Years of ethics training can be undone in a matter of minutes when organizational members see that their leaders don't practice what they preach.

■ *How to propose improvement ideas.* Organizations are full of creative people. They're always discovering new and improved ways of doing things. You don't even have to ask people to find improvements; they'll generally do it on their own. What the organization does have to do is provide a way to communicate and standardize improvements. One person with an excellent method is nice, but when everyone has adopted that excellent method, it has enormous implications.

Suggestion systems are one way to formally solicit people's ideas for improvement. (For information on suggestion systems, see my book,

The Continual Improvement Process: From Strategy to the Bottom Line, Paton Press, 2004). A simple open-door policy can also be a tool for organizational members to communicate their ideas to leadership. Whatever the method, train employees to seek improvements and communicate them once they're found. And make sure they think about improvements from their customers' perspective.

■ *Document control.* This might seem like an unusual training topic to drive customer focus. However, document control has a huge effect on customer loyalty. It's a process that's invisible to most customers, but they're directly affected by its effectiveness. Think about how many errors result from someone having the wrong specification, requirements, order, or instruction. Having the correct information is nothing more than document control. All employees should receive training on the organization's process for document control, including how documents can be revised, who approves revisions, where the current versions of documents are located, and what to do with obsolete documents.

These ten topics are by no means the only training issues that affect customers. Depending on the nature of your organization, there may be others. Put yourself in your customers' shoes and think about the kinds of training you'd expect organizational members to have. Even better, ask a few customers about the kind of training they'd like to see you provide your people. The ideas they come up with might surprise you. Keep the training focused on issues that affect the customer, and you can't go too far off course.

CHAPTER 9

Getting to Know Your Customers

P eople often long for the good old days of customer service. This longing always confuses me. After all, the range of product availability today is unsurpassed. A product or service can be delivered almost anywhere in the world in the wink of an eye. To top it all off, the prices of many goods and services are lower in relative terms than they've ever been. How can anyone long for a different time than this one? The developed world lives within a cornucopia of unmatched plenty, yet customers are still unsatisfied.

I asked a variety of people what they believe is lacking in their customer experiences. Most believe that their needs and expectations really aren't known by the organizations that serve them. The specific comments vary in nature, but they all point to a feeling of not being known and understood. Here are some of the remarks I've heard that point in this direction:

- "Years ago, people who I did business with knew my name. Not anymore. They couldn't care less who I am."
- "Just when I finally succeed in teaching someone how to service our account, they get a new person and the process starts all over again. They ought to pay me for training their employees."
- "Getting help in that place is like pulling teeth. If I was on fire, they probably wouldn't bother to throw water on me."
- "I don't want a hug every time I do business with them, but it would be nice to feel appreciated."
- "That company views me as a nuisance instead of as a customer who pays their salaries."

- "They change their services without any regard to what I really need as a customer."

These comments underscore a profound misunderstanding of the organizations' roles in serving their customers. You can talk about customer service all day, but talk rarely instills a real appreciation for the customer. Instead of talking about your customers, get to know them. When you know your customers, you want to do everything you can to help them. If you don't know them, they just become a nameless horde of distractions.

So the question is: How does an organization really get to know its customers? Let's begin with focus groups, a tool that can be applied to both existing and potential customers.

FOCUS GROUPS

A focus group brings together a small group of people (usually fewer than ten) to explore perceptions about a particular good, service, policy, or idea. The point is to concentrate on a short list of issues and explore them in detail. A facilitator is present to keep the group's discussions moving in the right direction and to ensure the details are recorded. The information garnered from the focus group is typically qualitative: threads of subjective observations about the issue being probed.

The power of a focus group lies in its ability to leverage multiple channels of communication and thought. This is similar to a brainstorming session, which also uses varied chains of thought to drill down and focus on an issue. Because a focus group relies on the interaction of its participants for success, two planning variables are critical:

- Using a skilled facilitator who can manage the group dynamics. Anyone who has ever presided over a free-flowing discussion knows how difficult this can be.
- Selecting participants who are willing and able to interact in a constructive manner. This often means selecting participants with somewhat similar backgrounds and/or demographics. It can be difficult to encourage lively interaction among participants who are uncomfortable being in one another's company.

In general, certain people shouldn't be asked to participate in the same focus group. These potential adversaries include bosses and subordinates, people in competition with one another, family members, experts and novices, and those who hold drastically different opinions from other participants. Participants won't be fully engaged in the focus group if they're intimidated or unduly influenced by others in the group.

Because the participants are carefully selected, the perceptions that come out of the focus group aren't a statistically valid representation of the population as a whole. This is the opposite of a quantitative survey, which strives for random selection of participants and statistical validity. There's nothing wrong with deliberate selection as long as decision makers are aware of it and don't try to base their decisions on the results of a single focus group. By their very nature, a focus group will represent what a fairly narrow slice of the population thinks about the issue being explored.

Participants are informed ahead of time about the general topic that will be addressed by the group but not the specific issues. For example, instead of saying that the group will focus on potato chips, participants might be told that they'll address snack foods. Why this secrecy about specific issues of exploration? Because many participants will research the subject if they know it ahead of time. This is human nature: Everyone wants to be as knowledgeable as possible. Unfortunately, it can also influence their thoughts and opinions during the focus group, resulting in flawed information for the researchers.

The lines of questioning in a focus group are exploratory, providing plenty of room for participants to stretch out and explore the topic from various angles. Typical lines of questioning include:

- What do you like about this product/policy/idea?
- What do you dislike?
- How does it compare to other products/policies/ideas?
- What would you change about it?

The interaction with other participants will branch out of these initial thoughts, and each of these questions could easily spawn a number of more detailed discussions. In fact, that's very desirable. The point is to start in a comfortable, generalized manner that allows participants to become familiar with the topic and each other, then drill down and focus on the details.

Participants might be surprised by their own thoughts and opinions on a subject, particularly when a skilled moderator encourages the group to dig deeper into the qualities under discussion. The facilitator's skill is critical at this juncture because a session that never produces anything more than generalities won't benefit anyone. Failing to achieve focus within the group suboptimizes the resulting information.

The results of the focus group are typically captured through electronic recording devices. Audio recorders and/or video cameras are almost essential, especially in recording the exact emotions, opinions, interactions, and hot buttons that arise from the group. Participants quickly forget about the presence of recording devices, and they soon ease into free-flowing discussions. Experienced and skilled facilitators often capture relevant points with a flipchart and marker, but this rarely works as well as an actual recording device. Using flipcharts and markers helps the facilitator guide the group's direction in a visual manner that everyone can follow. It's easier for participants to focus on the subject if they can also see what they're talking about.

Participating in a lively focus group can consume a considerable amount of energy. For this reason, this isn't an activity than can go on all day. People just can't keep up the intensity level. In addition, everyone worth inviting to your focus group will already be very busy. In general, focus groups run for two hours or less; however, they can occasionally run longer. Also, it's quite common for participants to be compensated in some way for their time and trouble. Meals, cash payments, product samples, souvenirs, and discounts may be used to motivate participation.

When the focus group has completed its work, everyone should be heartily thanked. The facilitator should do a quick review of the information that has been recorded, especially if any recording was performed manually. Memories are short, and the facilitator won't remember what cryptic notes mean a week after the focus group took place. Clarify all the details while the issues are still fresh in your mind. If electronic recording devices are used, make sure to turn them off, secure them, and remove the recording media. Don't make the mistake of leaving the videotape on top of the recorder. If observers were present during the focus group, it's often helpful for them to compare notes and impressions immediately after the group has adjourned.

Deborah Holden of Atlanta, Georgia, is a trained focus group moderator who has led numerous focus groups during her career. For a technical
audience, she said that focus groups are primarily engines for generating
ideas. "Focus groups are especially good at generating ideas early in the
product-development cycle, when it's too expensive or complex to develop
multiple prototypes," she explained. "The ideas that are gathered from the
focus group can then be explored further through quantitative techniques
before any big decisions are made."

Holden also outlined a couple of possible problems with focus groups.
"They're not particularly good at getting to the truth with politically correct questions," she explained. "If participants know the so-called 'right'
answer, they'll probably give it, even though it isn't an accurate representation of their thoughts and practices. This often comes up with focus groups
that address health, fitness, and nutrition. Few people will reveal the truth
on these issues in front of a bunch of strangers."

Finally, Holden cautioned facilitators to be on the lookout for the lone
"expert" that might emerge in a focus group. You most likely won't even
know who this is until the focus group is underway. "It's been my experience that an expert will try to take over the group," she said. "The group
interaction is harmed as participants become afraid of saying something
the expert might disagree with. In extreme situations, the expert can be
removed from the focus group. A domineering expert simply impedes the
natural group dynamics."

Focus groups can help the organization focus on issues and attributes
that will drive customer loyalty. Once the value proposition has been tailored to these issues and attributes, the organization should be ready to
start serving its customers. This typically starts with taking an order.

CAPTURING CUSTOMER REQUIREMENTS
ACCURATELY AND EFFICIENTLY

When customers place orders, it's critical that the organization have
a lean, efficient process for capturing customer requirements. A significant number of problems in many organizations can be traced to miscommunications at the point of placing the order. It all comes down to

that dangerous word "assume." We assumed we knew what the customer wanted. Of course, assumptions like this are often wrong. The amount of detail solicited from the customer at the time of the order shouldn't be a function of the order taker's natural curiosity. The detail must be standardized, so that the same variables are probed for all customers. Some people might think, "But this is only going to add time and effort to the process. Isn't that the opposite of lean?" In the short term, it might add time and effort. But in the long term, it will save invaluable time and effort. Remember: When an organization assumes it knows its customer requirements, complaints often result. These are expensive and time-consuming to address, so anything that prevents customers from having a bad experience is worthwhile.

It's helpful to divide customer requirement variables into two categories: product requirements and service requirements. It's also important to acknowledge that many of the so-called requirements are nothing more than desires, expectations, and preferences. These have the weight of requirements, and they must be treated as such whenever practical. The trick is to establish a lean process for capturing and comprehending all the desires, expectations, and preferences expressed by customers. Here are some of the potential lines of exploration for order takers:

Services
- Description of services to be performed
- Estimated cost, if known
- Date and time for services
- Contact person at customer location (including telephone or e-mail)
- Preferred sequence or priority of services, if applicable
- Waste disposal preferences, if applicable (e.g., on-site, off-site, or recycle)
- Desirability of expediting services (and willingness to pay additional costs, if any)
- Billing address
- Preferred service person

Goods

- Description of goods to be provided
- Additional features, services, or add-ons
- Estimated cost
- Date of delivery
- Packaging and labeling requirements
- Shipping requirements (e.g., contract carriers, customer pickup, or courier service)
- Partial order shipment OK?
- Exact shipping address
- Billing address

The best way to capture these requirements is through a standardized form. This can be paper or electronic, but the form's content should be consistent for all personnel using it. It should be revised when new variables are determined and old ones lose their relevance.

Once the requirements are determined, it's critical to briefly reconfirm the requirements to make sure that all details are accurate. Many organizations even fax or e-mail the documented order to customers for their confirmation. This practice is especially desirable when the order requirements are complex or the price high, but the ease of e-mail makes it applicable to almost any order. It's a wise preventive measure that can save a lot of time and trouble.

Asking customers to enter their own order requirements through the Internet can streamline the process as well. There are two important caveats to this approach:

- The order-entry procedure must be error-proofed and very simple. Don't rely on your customers' detail orientation and carefulness.
- For customers who prefer not to enter orders themselves or who don't trust the technology, provide another method for placing orders.

Questions are bound to come up during the order process, and there's nothing more frustrating (or inefficient) than a company representative who doesn't have the answers. The response, "I'll have to get back with you on that" should only be uttered as a last resort. Every person taking orders or interacting with customers should be an experienced user of the product or service being sold. Where possible, the order taker should be an experienced user under similar conditions to those that the customer will face. It's also desirable for the salesperson or order taker to have experience in producing or manufacturing the product. Someone with experience making the product and who's also experienced using it is in an especially good position to capture all the order details and answer questions on the spot.

GET TO KNOW YOUR CUSTOMERS PERSONALLY

Dale Carnegie's book, *How to Win Friends and Influence People* (Pocket Books, 1981) introduced the realities of human nature to the masses. That is, everybody thinks that he or she is the most important person in the world. Isn't that the way you feel? Your troubles are the most pressing, your triumphs the most tremendous, your challenges the most daunting, your interests the most riveting; and your loved ones the most special. These truths hold for your customers as well. Your customers think that what they're working on are the most critical tasks imaginable. They don't care what you're doing or what you're interested in. It's just human nature.

Your organization must take a personal interest in every customer and potential customer. As Carnegie first pointed out in 1936, this must be done sincerely. It's still true today. You can't seem premeditated or false in your interest. You've got to be truly interested in the customer. However, there's nothing wrong with using a tool to help you focus. Most organizations have hundreds (if not thousands) of customers, and keeping them all straight requires smart, lean tools. One particularly smart tool is the customer profile sheet. This is nothing more than what its name implies: an up-to-date profile of the customer's projects, products, interests, hobbies, family members, and other salient details. This isn't intrusive meddling. These are the issues that your customers care about, and they'll be happy that you care about them also. The information must be captured in a smooth, incremental manner, a little at a time. For instance, you might never learn about a client's children, but you might learn that this client is an avid fly fisherman. Capture whatever details you can and revise the information as it changes. The profile will grow into a database to help prompt you when conversing with the customer.

Prior to speaking with a customer, pull up his or her customer profile sheet and remind yourself of the thing that was on the customer's mind the last time you spoke. Ask him or her about this—whether it was fly-fishing, Girl Scouts, running, or volunteering for charities—and you'll create a strong bond with your customer. Remember: Your interest must be genuine. Hopelessly self-centered or cynical people shouldn't attempt this human relations technique until they've overcome their own personality quirks. A good way to help people break outside their own little worlds is to remind them that customers are the reason they're employed. For the organization's survival and the preservation of everybody's job, there's nothing more important than customers and their interests.

Of course, the customer profile sheet has more practical benefits, too. Knowing your customers' projects, products, customers, location, and organizational philosophies will help you guide them to the correct products and services. Empathize with your customers' challenges, and then propose solutions offered by your organization. You're adding value to your customer interaction by bringing with you a deeper understanding of your customers' needs and expectations. If your organization does this and your competitor doesn't, which one do you think has the edge?

The customer profile sheet's components could comprise almost anything. Here are some typical pieces of information that could be featured:

- Company name
- Location
- Local sports teams
- Preferred method of contact (e.g., phone, e-mail, fax)
- Last products purchased
- Special requests
- Current projects or products
- Current challenges and obstacles
- Primary customers and applications
- Primary contact person
- Contact's birthday
- Spouse's name

- Children's names
- Pets, if any (especially for customers without children)
- Interests and hobbies

A sample customer profile sheet is shown in appendix H. The profile can be a paper copy or electronic file, but there are distinct advantages to the electronic version, particularly in terms of fast and easy accessibility.

One caveat to using a customer profile sheet: The person using it must have had prior contact with the customer, at least with regard to the personal information. If a friend or acquaintance asks about daughter Judy, it's touching and thoughtful. If a stranger asks about Judy, it's alarming and inappropriate (and could be a cause for contacting law enforcement). Use good sense with this tool. The best application is to make individual employees responsible for maintaining profiles of their regular customers, and to encourage these same employees to use and update the profiles frequently.

GET TO KNOW YOUR CUSTOMERS BY SEEING THEM

The world is a busy and far-flung place. People barely have enough time to see their families, let alone anybody else. However, making time to interact with your customers is a valuable tool. It's also one of the best business investments you can make. If carefully scheduled and planned, it isn't that difficult or expensive to pull off.

Inviting select customers to visit your operation puts a personal face on the organization's work. It also drives discipline among team members because nobody wants to appear sloppy and disorganized in their customer's eyes. When I worked in manufacturing, plant tours were a regular occurrence. They had a sort of reawakening effect on management and staff that lasted for days afterward. Everybody realized that the customers were the people who relied on our work. Suddenly the work became personal and carried real consequences.

Facility tours aren't just for manufacturers. Any kind of service operation can invite selected customers to tour its back offices. What if you can't interest real customers in making a visit? Then contact your local Boy Scout troop, elementary school, or vocational club. They'll almost certainly be interested. The effect on your operation will be the same or even greater. By inviting people to see your operation, you knock your employees out of their confining mental boxes. You don't want to disrupt or distract them, but you do want to highlight the fact that your organization has customers and other parties who are interested in its operations. A tour underscores the fact that everybody's efforts are key to the enterprise's success.

Two considerations related to facility tours must be weighed:

- *Confidentiality.* Before you invite anyone into your facility, make sure he or she isn't a competitor or potential competitor. Even for noncompetitors, there might be areas of your operation that should remain off limits because of proprietary technologies or processes.
- *Liability.* Check with your insurance carrier about its liability policies for conducting facility tours. Usually it isn't a problem, but you'll want to check on this ahead of time. Stay out of potentially unsafe areas of the facility, even if your insurance carrier doesn't have a problem with it.

Asking your customers to come to you is a fine idea, but it's also great to visit them. This is especially powerful if you provide a product that's processed, assembled, or converted by your customers. The objective of visiting your customers is to see how your products really look and perform under actual use. Sure, everybody hears about how the products are performing, but actually seeing them in action makes an incredible impression. Employees' work suddenly takes on a renewed significance when they see the effect it has on a customer's operations. Employees can see the satisfaction or dissatisfaction right on the customer's face.

Early in my career, I was the quality supervisor at a quartz glass manufacturing facility. One of my responsibilities was to inspect and "map" the usable glass in large ingots of quartz. The task was abstract at best because the ingots were usually about three feet square, and I had to guess at the exact location and depth of various defects I identified. Add the fact that this inspection often took place on Friday afternoons, and you have the formula for a haphazard process. I figured our customers would figure out what was really inside the ingot once they started cutting on it.

My perceptions were altered when I finally had the opportunity to visit a customer and see just how critical my maps of usable glass were. I'll never forget the look of frustration on the customer's face as he tried to reconcile the ingot map with the ingot itself. He really did rely on my map to determine his usage strategy. A haphazard map on my part meant that his job was immensely more difficult. From that time forward my work on the ingots took on new significance. It was personal. I completely understood the effect my actions had on the customer, and the quality of my work improved dramatically.

It all comes down to this fact: When customers are faceless and their reactions invisible, you really have no way of knowing whether you made the grade. Visiting your customers can reveal the truth in a way that's hard to forget.

GET TO KNOW YOUR CUSTOMERS
BY BECOMING ONE

One of the most revealing ways to learn about customer satisfaction is to experience being a customer firsthand. You can always speculate about what the customer experience is like, but until you've been on the receiving end of your own goods or services, you really don't know. That's the underlying theory behind the "undercover customer" concept: Go undercover and find out what it's like to be a customer.

This technique—also known as "mystery shopping"—is widely used in retail, restaurants, hotels, mail order, and car dealerships. Someone impersonates a customer on behalf of the organization, paying close attention to the product's quality. The so-called customer could be an employee of the organization or someone who's hired for this sole purpose. In either case, it's important that the people within the organization don't realize how and when the undercover customer will emerge. The point is to truly experience the transaction in the same way a normal customer would.

What sorts of attributes might be examined? These are some of the common variables:

■ Timeliness of service
■ Accuracy of information received

- Courtesy of personnel
- Efficiency of the fulfillment process
- Aggressiveness of sales personnel
- Conformity of the final product
- Adherence to organizational policies

The undercover customer technique is the only method I'm aware of that produces customer perceptions on a firsthand basis, and there's no doubt that the method can deliver valuable information. All other methods filter the customer encounter second- or thirdhand. With undercover customers, you actually see, hear, smell, touch, and live the experience, which provides pure, unadulterated information.

The organization walks a fine line with this method, however. The undercover customer concept can be perceived as a "big brother" type of tool, making employees feel like they're under a magnifying glass. This can destroy morale, motivation, and the ability to retain employees. Clearly, the emphasis must be on the system, processes, and procedures in the organization. Employees shouldn't think they're being persecuted; everyone must understand that the undercover customer process is about learning to become better at serving the customer, not about trying to get people in trouble.

Some states even require that undercover customers act under the supervision of a licensed private investigator. Statutes like this only reinforce the idea that this method is solely for performing surveillance on employees, which we've already established shouldn't be the case. It would be worth examining the laws in your state before implementing an undercover customer process.

A number of companies specialize in providing undercover customer services to companies. Shop'n Chek Worldwide is the world's largest mystery shopping firm, located in Norcross, Georgia (*www.shopnchek.com*). Steven Maskell, Shop'n Chek's director of sales and marketing, provided some valuable perspectives on the concept: "Mystery Shopping helps preserve and enhance the most valuable asset a company has: its brand integrity. A good mystery-shopping program will ensure that all goods and services delivered by the company are consistent with the branding. Ultimately, mystery shopping should provide reliable data on which a company can make decisions. This is much more than someone just keeping tabs on employees; it's a strategic function."

Maskell went on to describe the mystery shopping function in more detail, particularly how it drives consistency. "People usually have already made up their minds when they do business with a company," he said. "They chose to be customers and want to remain customers. The objective of mystery shopping is to make sure that everything about that experience is consistent with the customer's expectations. Consistency is the key."

Another professional mystery shopping firm is Mystique Shopper. (*www.mystiqueshopper.com*). I spoke to its founder and president, John Saccheri, about the concept. Saccheri stated that the mystery-shopping concept delivers two basic results:

- Reveal patterns that reflect on the effectiveness of the organization's processes.
- Enforce a certain level of discipline among personnel. When the boss is around, everyone is on his or her best behavior. When the mystery shopper is enlisted, the boss is always around.

Saccheri emphasized that the organization must analyze the trends and not take action on isolated incidents. "When problems occur, they're often system problems as opposed to people problems," he said. "Address the system, and people issues usually go away. Of course, it's occasionally the case when the problem is a person, and mystery shopping will reveal this fact."

The undercover customer's findings are often positive. It's a learning experience, and there are many opportunities to recognize people for good performances. "When the process is presented in a positive light, employees seem to enjoy and embrace the undercover customer concept," said Saccheri. "The trick is in the way management uses the results. As with any tool, this can backfire if it's used incorrectly."

It's possible for organizations to adopt the undercover customer concept without any outside assistance. The approach would seem simple enough: Simply use employees as the undercover customer. However, this method brings with it some special challenges. Here are a few potential problems:

- *Employees can be recognized.* They won't truly be undercover. Employees who are serving them will recognize the undercover customers, and this will affect their behavior. This isn't the circumstance in all cases, but it would be a serious consideration.

■ *Employees know how everything works.* Employees are more likely to work within the known constraints of the company, taking into consideration its weaknesses and obstacles. They're not likely to run into the potential snares that real customers might encounter.

■ *Employees have a hard time being objective.* Employees already know whom they like, whom they don't like, and the organization's problems. For these insiders, company politics are unavoidable. Third parties are more likely to approach the task in a more balanced, neutral manner.

The organization must design a tool for capturing undercover customer perceptions. This might include open-ended questions (What did you like? What did you dislike?), focused questions (Were you served within fifteen minutes?), scaled questions (Please rate the courtesy of your salesperson on a scale from one to five), or some mix of all of these. Clearly, the tool's design has its own challenges. As with so many other customer perception methods, it makes sense to begin simply (i.e., start with open-ended questions and basic focused questions), and then move on to more sophisticated ratings methodologies after the process matures.

To summarize, innumerable techniques are available for capturing customer perceptions. The approaches are limited only by your organization's powers of creativity. Doing a little research into what other companies have done also helps. Don't fall into the trap of thinking that a survey is the only valid tool. Call reports, field reports, comment cards, complaint systems, warranty analysis, after-order follow-ups, customer hospitality days, focus groups, and undercover customers can all deliver valuable information. Try a method and be prepared to switch gears when necessary. But no matter what methods you use, don't forget to take action on the results.

CHAPTER 10

Innovation Management

Innovation is a powerful driver of customer loyalty and long-term success. Not just any innovation, though—innovation that customers and potential customers deem valuable. Often, organizations mistakenly assume the market will embrace all their innovations enthusiastically. The back alleys of business are littered with innovations that nobody found necessary or useful. Failed innovations are among the most expensive mistakes an organization can make.

Organizations must objectively evaluate their ideas for innovation long before they're ever launched. The decision to embark on a new design must be supported with a great deal of clear-headed analysis. This takes discipline and effort but is more than rewarded in the long run. Once the decision is made to pursue an opportunity, the hard work of design begins. An organization must have a method for ensuring that the innovation's potential is realized by the ultimate product. Both of these major phases—idea management and design control—are part of something I call innovation management. The diagram in figure 10.1 summarizes the relationship between the various steps of innovation management.

Innovation management is really nothing more than taking a very complex process (i.e., initiating and designing a new product) and breaking it into a series of smaller, more manageable subprocesses. The subprocesses are linked in a logical manner so that the output of one activity becomes the input to the next one. Each of the smaller activities is monitored and managed, ensuring that the overall design process achieves the desired results. Deliberation and method are key.

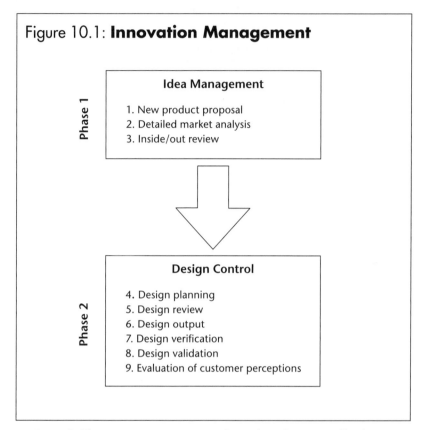

Figure 10.1: **Innovation Management**

Idea Management

Phase 1

1. New product proposal
2. Detailed market analysis
3. Inside/out review

Design Control

Phase 2

4. Design planning
5. Design review
6. Design output
7. Design verification
8. Design validation
9. Evaluation of customer perceptions

Remarkably, many organizations deny that they actually design or innovate anything, even when it's obvious they do. Why would an organization deny the existence of something that can be such a powerful tool? There are a number of reasons:

- Fear that formal innovation management will hinder creativity
- Fear that it will slow the design process down
- Assumption that innovation management is nothing more than mindless bureaucracy
- Misconception that designers and creative people won't tolerate any kind of structure
- Fear of being audited against the design requirements of a standard such as ISO 9001

All these reasons are misconceptions, of course. Innovation management actually facilitates creativity because it allows people to focus on each step of design. Time isn't wasted on reinventing the process each time a new design is proposed. Designs progress within a secure architecture of procedures that ensure each step meets the established criteria. The procedures introduce only as much control as is absolutely necessary. Far from slowing down the process, innovation management speeds up the process by removing roadblocks, errors, and miscommunications.

The most important principle of successful innovation management is it to keep it as simple as possible. Conceiving and designing a product is a complex endeavor, but the process used to manage design must be simple. If your design control process isn't intuitive and streamlined, then it might need to undergo a design change itself.

Let's begin our discussion of design by examining phase 1 of the process: idea management.

PHASE 1: IDEA MANAGEMENT

The term "idea management" sounds a little Orwellian. One can almost imagine the faceless voice of Big Brother declaring, "We must manage these ideas!" That's far from the intention, though. The objective of idea management is to make it easy to generate ideas. Provide a structured, simple way to propose new goods and services, and then submit all proposals to the same objective criteria. The organization benefits from having everyone engaged in proposing new and improved products. Limited resources dictate that only the best ideas are pursued, though.

Idea management is actually comprised of three stages:

1. *New product proposal:* Description of the idea along with a first evaluation of the proposal
2. *Detailed market analysis:* Exploration of the idea's potential using feedback from customers
3. *Inside/out review:* Comprehensive review of all factors related to the idea: technical, financial, marketing. This is the proposal's final evaluation prior to beginning any design work.

Each of the three stages builds on one another, gradually constructing a business case for the new product idea. Of course, each stage also requires evaluation and approval, so it's entirely possible that some ideas never even proceed past stage one of idea management.

New Product Proposal

New product proposal is the starting point for the entire process. It's an opportunity for anyone to say, "Hey, I have a neat product idea." The broader and more diverse the ideas, the better. Open the floodgates. Many of the ideas will fizzle out before they even get close to a customer, but that's OK. The strong ideas will receive more investigation, and the lesser ones will die a quiet death without consuming a lot of time and resources.

Once an idea is proposed by way of a new product proposal form as shown in appendix F, it's submitted to a series of questions that evaluate its potential for success. The questions include such issues as: "Does the new product fit in an existing product line?" and "Does the new product fit our current strategy?" For each question, a yes response is considered more favorable. The person proposing the idea should also answer the questions. This gives the initiator ownership over the idea and its initial evaluation. Depending on the number of yeses that result, the proposal will require different levels of approval to proceed, as indicated by the diagram in figure 10.2.

Figure 10.2: **Proposal Approval Scorecard**

Score	Guidance	Approvals needed to proceed to detailed market analysis
0–4	RED (danger, possible incompatibility, high risk)	CEO Vice president of innovation Director of sales
5–8	YELLOW (caution, moderate risk)	Vice president of innovation Director of sales
9–14	GREEN (attractive, favorable fit, synergies)	Director of sales

Nine to fourteen yeses indicate the proposal is a good fit with existing operations, and thus relatively low-risk. In the example shown, only the approval of the director of sales would be required to move the idea to stage two of the evaluation process. It's expected that the person approving the proposal will also provide some oversight over the question responses that are given to ensure that the proposal's initiator hasn't exaggerated its potential. Five to eight yeses are considered more risky, thus requiring more approvals—and the additional scrutiny that comes with them. Zero to four yeses on the new product proposal signal ideas with the highest risk and lowest compatibility. These ideas must receive approval at the highest levels before they qualify for more evaluation. In the example shown above, these ideas would require approval by the CEO.

The questions on the new product proposal form focus on compatibility with existing products, markets, and capabilities. In general, this can serve as an effective first cut for a new product idea. Organizations are often more successful when they innovate in their fields of expertise, as opposed to exploring completely new frontiers. By no means should ideas that are incompatible with existing products, markets, and capabilities be rejected automatically. But incompatible products should be held to higher scrutiny. If three top managers agree that the potential success outweighs the liabilities, then even so-called incompatible ideas proceed to the next stage.

Detailed Market Analysis

The second stage of idea management is detailed market analysis. This stage requires that the organization identify at least four potential customers for the new product. These customers are selected for their candor and impartiality. You don't want friendly confederates who will tell the organization what it wants to hear; you want the hard truth.

Each sampled customer is briefed about the new product proposal and then asked to respond to a series of statements about the idea. The responses are made according to a five-point scale, ranging from "strongly disagree" to "strongly agree," and all responses are recorded on the detailed market analysis form (shown in appendix G). The survey statements include such statements as: "We're likely to purchase this product," and "This product will help us be more successful." A set of five identical statements are included within the survey for each of the four customers, along with a handful of open-ended questions probing specific requirements from the customer's perspective.

The entire process should take no more than about five to ten minutes for each customer. The detailed market analysis could easily be administered via telephone, e-mail, mail, or in person. The usual rules apply to initiating this kind of mini-survey as to any other:

- Describe the purpose of the survey to the customer, which is to gauge the potential success of the new product idea.
- Explain that the customer's responses won't be construed as a commitment to purchase in the future.
- Explain that the survey won't take more than five or ten minutes.
- Assure the customer that all responses will be held in strict confidence.
- Ask the customer if he or she would mind taking a few minutes and participating.

Care must be taken when selecting whom to sample within the customer organization. Ideally, you don't want a purchasing manager, who happens to be one of the more accessible people. A technical or managerial professional who has firsthand experience with the type of product under consideration will be in a much better position to give reliable answers.

Why even go to the trouble of asking customers what they think about the new product idea? Because a customer will give you an external viewpoint, something that's lacking when it's most needed. Organizations are often very good at deluding themselves into thinking that ideas are much better than they really are. Including the perspectives of potential customers injects a dose of reality to the process. It's better to hear the truth early in the process than later, when resources have been consumed and people become emotionally invested in the idea.

The responses to the four interviews are summarized and an average response calculated for each question. It's important to realize that the average indicates a central tendency and nothing more. With only four customers being sampled, data resulting from this mini-survey are far from statistically significant. The averages are only a rough indication of what this small group of potential customers thought about the idea. It's a flawed sanity check, but it's better than none at all.

The level of approval required for the proposal is based on the lowest single average response. Any average response that falls between one and 2.9 indicates that the proposal might face very little market acceptance, and it will require the highest level of approval. Any average that falls between three and 3.9 indicates that the proposal faces uncertain market acceptance, which requires somewhat less stringent approval. Any average that falls between four and five indicates that there's market enthusiasm for the innovation. These proposals require even less approval to move to the next stage. Guidance on the necessary approvals is shown in figure 10.2.

Inside/Out Review

The inside/out review is the third and final stage of idea management. It's exactly what it sounds like: a comprehensive examination of all aspects of the new product idea. The inside/out review takes much of the information gleaned from the two earlier examinations and adds additional details. It's a "deep dive" into every angle of the proposal. Three major sections are included in the inside/out review:

1. *Business review:* Projected business effects of the new product, including sales, prices, revenue, and margins
2. *Technical review:* Performance and technical attributes of the new product, and the equipment and personnel competencies needed to produce it
3. *Marketing review:* Customer target segments, marketing angles, and effects on existing products

The inside/out review is the most detailed phase of idea management. In all likelihood, it will also require more time and effort to complete. Any idea that gets this far in the evaluation process has already been deemed to have serious potential, so the extra time and effort is probably worth it. The investment in the inside/out review is the organization's last opportunity to take a hard look at the proposal before beginning the design process.

Typically, the three sections of the inside/out review will be completed independently of one another, although they can certainly be combined.

The only caveat is that each section be given the time and attention needed to address it comprehensively. The inside/out review should be objective, sober, and supported by evidence. In fact, a significant amount of data and information might need to be attached to the review as supporting evidence.

The highest decision makers in the organization must approve the completed inside/out review. There are no quantitative thresholds for approving the proposal as there were with the earlier two evaluations. The inside/out review relies on the judgment of the approvers and their evaluation of the information provided. For this reason, the approver's role is much more important at this stage than at any other. It could also be said that the information-gatherer's role is more important during this stage as well. Let's inventory the responsibilities of both categories of personnel involved in the inside/out review.

Information gatherers:

- Complete the applicable sections of the inside/out review
- Support all conclusions with evidence
- Attach data and other information that clarify and add credibility to the review
- Don't allow their prejudices about the idea to influence their research
- Gather evidence in an even-handed and objective manner

Approvers:

- Actually *read* everything in the inside/out review. This isn't the time to gloss over details.
- Carefully review all conclusions and evidence, weighing the logic of everything
- Ask questions when anything seems contradictory or unusual
- Keep the customer's perspective in the forefront of their minds. The customer's perspective will ultimately determine if the idea becomes a success or failure.
- Only approve ideas that are so strong they'd invest their own money in them.

The bottom line of the inside/out review is that it involves a lot of work. Invest the effort, and the organization will be better prepared to develop a successful product that the market embraces. It's worth noting that the approved inside/out review contains the design inputs, which define exactly what requirements the design must fulfill. This is the first explicit link to ISO 9001.

A sample inside/out review form is shown in appendix H. This form's content could easily be customized to meet the needs of any organization, although the issues addressed in the sample will probably meet most enterprises' needs.

PHASE 2: DESIGN CONTROL

Ideas that have passed all three stages of idea management proceed to design control. This phase includes the actual steps of turning the new product idea into something tangible (i.e., a good and/or service that someone is willing to pay for). All the information learned during the idea management phase becomes input to the design process. In fact, this information will be referenced frequently during design so that the essential requirements aren't forgotten.

Design control is comprised of five stages. These match almost perfectly with the disciplines outlined in ISO 9001. The only differences are that design inputs are defined during an inside/out review, and the sequence of steps falls in a slightly different order:

1. *Design planning:* Laying out the specific steps, responsibilities, time frames, reviews, and deliverables that the design will involve
2. *Design review:* A check to make sure the design plan is proceeding according to expectations
3. *Design outputs:* Documents and other information that define exactly what the organization has designed
4. *Design verification:* A comparison of the design outputs against requirements defined in the inside/out review
5. *Design validation:* A check of the design output under conditions of actual use

6. *Product launch:* Rolling out the new product to market, a step that's frequently shortchanged

Let's take a look at each of these steps in more detail.

Design Planning

The design plan is simply the path you expect to take when creating the design. It's nothing more than your best guess at the way the process will proceed. Of course, plans are often wrong and don't guarantee any kind of success. Not having a design plan, however, will almost always guarantee failure.

The plan can take many forms, from highly sophisticated to very simple. The trick is to match the design plan to the nature of the product being designed. Some plans are little more than a memo or a flow diagram. For more complex products, the design plan could be comprised of many documents, including a Gantt chart, critical path, work breakdown structure, and other project management tools. Use only as much planning as you absolutely need. Remember: the purpose of design planning is to help you manage the design process. The tools you use to do this are completely up to you.

Design planning addresses a number of critical variables:

- *Participants and responsibilities:* Who exactly will be involved with this design? What will they be expected to do? Do the participants understand and accept their responsibilities?
- *Interfaces:* With whom should the persons with design responsibilities interface or interact? Nobody works in isolation (or at least they shouldn't), and it's important to drive as much communication and interaction as possible.
- *Resources:* What funds, facilities, equipment, supplies, and other resources will be needed to carry out this design? Have the resources been secured? If not, where will they come from?
- *Major tasks:* What major tasks must be performed to produce the design? In what sequence should these tasks be performed? Keep in mind that major tasks will include verifications and validations of the design, both of which are discussed later in this chapter.

- *Deliverables:* What are the deliverables or products of each task? How will you know the task has been accomplished?
- *Timing of tasks and deliverables:* When are tasks due to be completed? When will the deliverables be produced?
- *Reviews:* How will the organization review progress on the design? Who will be involved in the reviews? When will the reviews take place?
- *Verification(s):* Exactly what attributes of the design will be evaluated during design verification? How will the design be verified? Who will perform verification?
- *Validation(s):* What attributes, features, and performance properties of the design will be evaluated during validation? How will validation be performed? Who will perform it?

For some organizations, the design plan remains basically the same each time they design something. The only difference is the specific timing of the tasks. Organizations that design variations of the same kind of product can often recycle their design plans. For these cases, there's no reason to make the design plan any more complicated than it needs to be. A simple template such as the one presented in figure 10.3 works very well.

This is a highly simplified example, of course. Design planning may require significantly more documents, but smart organizations will keep their plans as simple and streamlined as possible. The tasks described in the plan will certainly need to be customized to an organization's circumstances and the product being designed. However, this general approach will work for many organizations.

Regardless of the form it takes, the design plan is a living document. It's subject to revision as you learn more about the specific design being addressed. Compare actual progress against the plan frequently, and make changes as necessary.

Design Review

Design reviews ensure that the design is proceeding according to plan. All designs should have at least one design review, and complex designs might have many more. In the sample design plan shown in fig. 10.3, there

Figure 10.3: **Sample Design Plan**

Task	Responsibility	Interfaces	Due date
1. Analyze inside/out review (design inputs)	Lead designer Engineering manager	Production manager	
2. Finalize technical specification	Engineering manager	Lead designer Purchasing manager	
3. Create drawing	Lead designer	Purchasing manager Engineering manager	
4. Verification against inside/out review criteria	Engineering manager Lead designer	Production manager	
5. First design review	Engineering manager Lead designer	Production manager Purchasing manager Vice president of operations	
6. Produce prototype	Lead designer	Production manager	
7. Prototype verification	Engineering manager	Production manager Lead designer	
8. Mold created	Purchasing manager Molding subcontractor	Production manager	
9. Design validation (first article inspection)	Lead designer Customer	Production manager	
10. Final design review	Lead designer Engineering manager	Production manager Purchasing manager Vice president of operations President	
11. Parts released for production	Production manager	Engineering manager	
12. Parts delivered to customer	Salesperson	Production manager Scheduling coordinator	

are two design reviews: one occurs about midway through the design process, and the other near the end. There's no "right" number of design reviews. If the design process has a great deal of complexity and risk, then obviously there will need to be more reviews. A key planning activity is to decide how many design reviews are appropriate for the particular product being designed.

People who participate in design reviews are those who are involved in the design stage being reviewed. Typical participants include designers, engineers, production managers, purchasing personnel, and logistics managers. Later in the design process, reviews could also include marketing, sales, and senior management. The point is to get the people who understand the design variables together and review the status of all the design tasks. The review doesn't have to be a physical meeting but could occur as a teleconference or through other remote means. As long as the participants have access to necessary information relating to the design's progress, then it doesn't really matter if everyone is together in the same room. Face-to-face dialogue can be helpful, however, especially when problems must be resolved.

Each design review should be conducted according to a structured agenda. Don't leave the content of a review up to the participants' discretion. Publish the agenda in advance and make sure all participants are prepared to contribute.

The following actions are usually addressed during a design review:

- Evaluation of progress on the design
- Comparison of progress against the design plan
- Agreement on actions needed to close gaps
- Identification of resources to be procured or realigned
- Revision of the design plan, if necessary
- Feedback and encouragement to designers
- Identification of risks and roadblocks that have appeared, and decisions made about how they'll be managed
- Confirmation that the design is ready to move on to the next stage
- Confirmation that the design is focused on the requirements identified during the inside/out review

The design review is a reality check to ensure that everything is on track. For activities that aren't on track or don't meet requirements, corrective actions are agreed upon and implemented. Design reviews must be action-oriented to be effective. Because action lies at the heart of the design review, it's necessary to maintain and distribute records of the reviews.

Design Output

Design output is exactly what it sounds like: the output of the design process. This defines exactly what the organization will produce to meet the design input requirements, which are summarized on the inside/out review form. Design output always takes the form of documentation of some sort. Here are some examples:

- Sketches
- Engineering drawings
- Blueprints
- Product specifications
- Service instructions
- Bills of materials
- Manufacturing instructions
- Installation instructions
- Specifications for components, subassemblies, raw materials, or other purchased products
- Packaging and labeling specifications
- Handling and storage specifications
- Appearance standards
- Safety warnings, labels, and reminders
- Consumer or user instructions
- Troubleshooting and repair guides
- Flowcharts
- Calculations
- Computer code
- Operating criteria
- Physical specimens or prototypes

The possible format and style of design outputs are limited only by the organization's imagination. But regardless of what they look like, there are a number of requirements that must be met:

1. *Approval and revision status:* Design outputs provide current information to the organization, which means they must be treated as documents. The two most applicable components of document control are approval and revision statuses. Approval simply means someone has evaluated the outputs and determined they're adequate. The revision status, of course, indicates what version the outputs represent, and it's typically reflected by a date, letter, or number. Approval and revision statuses for the outputs will apply even if the output isn't a traditional document. When outputs are changed or enhanced, they're revised just like any other document. It's important to note that design outputs are often formally approved after they're submitted for design verification (see the section following).

2. *Satisfaction of input requirements:* The whole point of design outputs is to guide the organization in producing a new or improved product. To do this, outputs must clearly meet the input requirements. We've defined our primary "design input" as the inside/out review, so it's critical that this document be referenced as the outputs are generated. All relevant requirements outlined by the inside/out review must be satisfied within the output(s). This has a great deal of value because it ensures that the organization pays attention to the expectations of its customers and the marketplace as it goes through the design process.

3. *Provide information to all relevant functions:* Design outputs are communication tools. Their primary function is to tell everyone what they must do to make the new product a success. As such, they must provide information to functions such as purchasing, logistics, production, quality assurance, and sales. That's one of the reasons there might be multiple design outputs: They're tailored to a wide variety of functions.

4. *Include acceptance criteria:* The outputs must indicate what constitutes acceptable product attributes. In other words, what specific requirements must the product meet? Among many possible issues, examples of acceptance criteria include dimensional tolerances, performance

specifications, material properties, and aesthetic requirements. The nature of the product clearly dictates what kind of acceptance criteria will apply. Note that acceptance criteria apply not only to the design of goods, but also to the services the organization designs.

5. *Provide guidance on safe and proper use:* Customers are often creative in the way they use products, especially new products. Occasionally they even use products inappropriately in ways that lead to injury or death. The design outputs must clearly indicate the safe and appropriate use of the product. Doing this protects the organization *and* its customers. Organizations that fail to perform this step with due diligence often find themselves facing costly lawsuits, bankruptcy, and criminal prosecution.

Design Verification

During design verification, design outputs are checked against the design inputs to ensure all input requirements have been met. (See the inside/out review in appendix H.) It's basically an inspection activity, but it's also one of the most critical inspections that an organization can perform. Verification can be performed once near the end of the design process, or it may be done multiple times as incremental design outputs are generated. It all depends on the product being designed. Complex products will almost always require more than one design verification.

Verification is more challenging than it would first appear. It's an abstract task because the thing being verified is usually a representation of the product—a drawing, for instance—rather than the product itself. People performing design verification must examine attributes shown on the output documents and ensure that they meet the input requirements' full intent and scope. This is typically more than just a simple check. Here are some examples that provide an idea of the range of design verification:

- *Confirmation of basic attributes:* This is the most routine type of verification. It simply involves comparing the requirements shown on design inputs against the attributes reflected on the output documents. Attributes that can be verified in this manner might include size, shape, weight, color, and configuration.
- *Verification of performance properties:* This is a more robust type of verification. Performance properties may include speed, strength, hard-

ness, durability, reliability, and other qualities. Typically these can't be checked off mechanically like basic attributes; calculations, simulations, or computer modeling might be needed to determine whether the performance requirements in the inputs have been satisfied by the outputs. Keep in mind that these performance properties are shown on design output documents.

- *Tests of prototypes:* Design outputs sometimes include prototypes of the product being designed. In these cases, verification might include actual tests of the prototype's physical properties. This represents a shift away from verifying documents to verifying something the customer would recognize as a real product. The way the prototype differs from a real product, though, is that it's not produced under typical production conditions. Prototypes are produced under careful conditions probably unlike those that will be present when the design goes into full production. Nevertheless, testing the prototype can still provide valuable insights.

- *Comparison to similar designs from the past:* History is a powerful source of knowledge, although it's often overlooked. When verifying design outputs, it's helpful to refer to earlier designs that have similar attributes and performance properties. How well does the current design shape up to designs of the past? Does it incorporate all the lessons learned from the earlier designs? Is there customer feedback on earlier designs that should be incorporated into the current design?

- *Safety and health review:* Verification should carefully consider the safety and health aspects of the product being designed. The design inputs will provide direction on applicable considerations, but sometimes it's difficult early in the process to know with certainty what safety and health issues apply. For that reason, design verification should apply as wide a range of all possible safety and health issues as possible to ensure that nothing has been neglected. Unsafe or unhealthy products will doom the organization, no matter how innovative the products are.

- *Environmental impact review:* Every product used or produced by mankind has an environmental impact. It's a truth that's beyond argument. The question isn't whether the new product causes environmental impacts, but how severe they are. Design outputs must be verified to ensure they meet all applicable environmental laws. Just as important, outputs should be verified to ensure that unregulated effects aren't being generated in excess quantities. A full life-cycle review of the product, its packaging, and the associated supplies is a responsible way to verify the environmental effect of the product being designed.

■ *Marketing review:* Nearly everything mentioned so far about design verification has been technical in nature. It's important not to lose sight of the design's purpose: to meet a need in the marketplace. The organization's marketing specialists should be involved in the design verification to ensure that nothing identified in the design inputs are forgotten, particularly in the case of subtle or highly nuanced requirements.

■ *Legal review:* In the United States, a company can be sued for almost anything. Grounds for filing suit range from the gravely serious to the ridiculous. The very nature of a new or improved product means an organization is venturing into a potentially risky and untried area of operation. Many product designs require input from legal staff so that these risks are managed properly.

Any qualified persons inside or outside the organization can perform design verification. Due to the confidential nature of most designs, however, verifications are typically performed inside the organization. Regardless of where the verifications take place, it's helpful if the verification is performed by an independent function. At the very least, avoid having designers verify their own work. A fresh set of eyes will always reveal new insights.

There's always the chance that design verification will result in changes to the design. And that's really the point: to ensure that the design meets all requirements, and if not, to make necessary changes. Changes can be triggered by any number of factors:

■ Failure to address input requirements
■ Misinterpretation of input requirements
■ Unsatisfactory test or simulation results
■ Errors or omissions in the design
■ Addition of lessons learned from earlier designs
■ Unanticipated or unmet safety and/or health considerations

- Unanticipated or unmet environmental considerations
- Significant legal risks
- Addition of improved features or performance attributes

That last bullet is a potential danger zone. It's possible that competitive realities may drive midstream changes during the design process. The organization must be careful not to make the design a constantly moving target. Frequent changes to the design are expensive, time-consuming, and often contrary to the spirit of the original ideas that initiated the design in the first place.

Design verification always produces records. These indicate who performed the verification, when it was performed, what specific parameters were verified, the results of the verification, and any actions that must be taken. The records can be quite simple and are often incorporated into other design records.

Design Validation

Validation is similar to verification except that an actual version of the product is evaluated rather than abstract representations of the product (e.g., drawings and specifications). The product may be a production prototype, sample, beta test, pilot run, or first article, but essentially it's the same product that will be offered to customers. Validation sums up everything about the designed product and asks the question, "Will this product do everything it's supposed to do in the eyes of the customer?"

These are the four keys to successful validation:

1. Evaluate the same product that customers will actually use.
2. Evaluate the product in the same way customers will use or misuse it.
3. Evaluate the product in a holistic or cumulative manner instead of focusing only on product attributes isolated from one another.
4. Evaluate the production process to ensure it's truly capable of producing the new product.

Don't make the mistake of validating a product that was produced by experts under carefully controlled conditions in a research and design laboratory. The validated product must be produced in the same way it's produced for market consumption. All the typical production problems that arise when a product goes into day-to-day production should be considered. The organization certainly shouldn't cherry-pick its best materials, personnel, and equipment when producing a product for validation. The production conditions should be realistic.

In fact, the product must be both produced and evaluated under realistic conditions. Thus, if you're designing golf carts, you'd take a cart for a spin on an actual golf course and put up with the rain, shine, heat, and cold just as a real golfer might. The organization must also try to anticipate ways the customer might misuse the product. Perhaps the golf cart isn't really designed to be driven through three inches of standing water, but that's exactly what golfers will do. Golfers might also be expected to drive the cart over curbs and other obstructions, or spill beer on the seats and dashboard. Validation must include all of these uses and misuses.

Validation evaluates individual product features, but more important, it summarizes all the features and determines if the product as a whole meets requirements. Everyone has heard the cliché, "More than a sum of its parts." The designed product is much more than a sum of its parts, and the validation should acknowledge this. The overall perceptions of the persons performing validation often are more valuable than the results of individual evaluations.

If the product is the sort that customers will submit to quality control or acceptance testing prior to use, then validation must also include the same type of testing. Products with published specifications (e.g., strength, elongation, speed, dimensions, and temperature) are almost always submitted to some sort of inspection by customers, even if the supplier performs the inspections on their behalf. Validation is the time to learn about any potential problems with these acceptance tests. Actually, verification was the right time, but at that point the organization might not have had access to a real product to test.

Here are some examples of how different products undergo validation:

- Medicine: clinical trials
- Educational course: beta tests using volunteer students
- Automobiles: road test trials, crash test trials, and engineering tests
- Food and beverages: taste tests with consumers, laboratory tests
- Kitchen appliances: multiple-cycle usage tests, consumer focus group

Strive to get real customers involved in design validation. Some types of validation, such as crash tests, obviously aren't appropriate for direct customer participation, but many others are. Customers are especially good at looking past isolated performance attributes and individual test results. They tend to evaluate the design in its entirety, taking into consideration factors that the organization might have missed. That fresh perspective is what you want included in your validations.

Be creative when you develop your validation criteria. Yes, you're validating the *intended use* of the design, but to achieve true customer loyalty, sometimes you've got to predict some *reasonable foreseeable uses*. This isn't to say an organization must plan for everything a customer might do, but it should realize that customers could stretch the limits of what a product was designed for. Should they? Of course not. Will they? Yes, and they'll hold the organization responsible for any perceived failures of the design, even if the failures are their own fault.

The organization has two choices:

- Error-proof its design so customers can't invent unintended uses.
- Acknowledge that customers will twist the intended uses and try to plan for these twists.

When the twists introduce safety, health, environmental, or legal risks, the organization has no choice but to error-proof the design. When these risks aren't present, the organization should plan for reasonable unintended uses. The best way to learn about these is to get customers intimately involved in the validation process.

Smart organizations not only validate the design, but also the support materials associated with it. These include:

- Packaging
- Labeling
- Safety and health warnings

Just like verification, validation produces records. These should outline all the details of the validation: the manner of validation, conditions under which it took place, exactly what features or attributes were validated, who performed it, and when it took place. The typical rules of records apply here: Keep them simple and as concise as possible.

Design validation is one of the most important activities in the design control process because it forces the organization to perform a reality check on its design work. Validation requires a deliberate, head-to-head examination of what the organization designed versus the customer's use in the real world. Spend the time and effort to perform a comprehensive design validation. The diligence will pay dividends.

Evaluation of Customer Perceptions

You launch the product and your work is done, right? Wrong. A process must be established to proactively capture and evaluate customer perceptions of the new product. The process doesn't necessarily have to be separate from routine capturing of customer perceptions on existing products, but many organizations develop separate systems for their new products. It really doesn't matter as long as the system is in place and is fully implemented.

A robust innovation management process ensures that good ideas follow the long and sometimes bumpy road to customer loyalty. Innovation management is the vehicle that carries the organization to future success. If your organization won't drive that vehicle to successful innovation, some other organization will.

APPENDICES

Customer Focus Inventory

Customer Feedback

Strongly agree   Disagree   Neutral   Agree   Strongly disagree

	-2	-1	0	1	2
1. Customer feedback is shared with employees at all levels.	☐	☐	☐	☐	☐
2. Most customer feedback is captured proactively.	☐	☐	☐	☐	☐
3. We always take action on trends in customer feedback.	☐	☐	☐	☐	☐
4. We tell customers about improvement we've made as a result of their feedback.	☐	☐	☐	☐	☐
5. We take action on customer feedback as soon as possible after receiving it.	☐	☐	☐	☐	☐
6. Capturing customer feedback isn't an "event" in our organization; we do it all the time.	☐	☐	☐	☐	☐

Top Management

7. Top management frequently communicates the importance of the customer.	☐	☐	☐	☐	☐
8. Top management consistently exhibits customer focus in its daily actions and decisions.	☐	☐	☐	☐	☐

Strongly agree Disagree Neutral Agree Strongly disagree

-2   -1   0   1   2

9. Top management takes a genuine interest in the
    organization's employees and their well-being....... ☐ ☐ ☐ ☐ ☐

10. Customer satisfaction metrics are included in our
    organization's key measures. .... ☐ ☐ ☐ ☐ ☐

11. Meetings of top management frequently include
    analysis and action on customer feedback. .... ☐ ☐ ☐ ☐ ☐

12. The top three causes of customer complaints are
    known by top management...................... ☐ ☐ ☐ ☐ ☐

13. Measurements of top management performance
    include customer loyalty and/or customer
    satisfaction. .... ☐ ☐ ☐ ☐ ☐

Complaints

14. Team problem solving is utilized to address customer
    complaints. .... ☐ ☐ ☐ ☐ ☐

15. Our organization never views a complaint as a
    nuisance..................................... ☐ ☐ ☐ ☐ ☐

16. We always verify that corrective actions taken on
    complaints are effective........................ ☐ ☐ ☐ ☐ ☐

17. The status of customer complaints, including
    corrective actions, is communicated throughout the
    organization................................. ☐ ☐ ☐ ☐ ☐

Strongly agree
Disagree
Neutral
Agree
Strongly disagree

18. We view customer complaints as learning
opportunities. . . . .
  -2 -1 0 1 2
□ □ □ □ □

19. We try to make it convenient for customers to
complain. . . . .
□ □ □ □ □

20. Ineffective actions on complaints are viewed as
serious threats to our survival. . . . .
□ □ □ □ □

21. Root cause analysis is vigorously enforced on
customer complaints. . . . .
□ □ □ □ □

General Awareness
□ □ □ □ □

22. Personnel throughout the organization know who
their customers are, both internal and external. . . . . .
□ □ □ □ □

23. Personnel through the organization can communicate
how their actions affect customers. . . . .
□ □ □ □ □

24. Employees at all levels of the organization know how
customers use our products. . . . .
□ □ □ □ □

25. Nobody in our organization would claim he or she
doesn't have a customer. . . . .
□ □ □ □ □

26. Customer-service success stories are shared widely
throughout the organization. . . . .
□ □ □ □ □

27. Customer tours in our facility are a regular
occurrence. . . . .
□ □ □ □ □

Strongly agree
                                      Disagree
                                        Neutral
                                          Agree
                                            Strongly disagree
                                      -2 -1   0   1   2

28. Our personnel often visit customer locations to
    observe our products in use. . . . . □ □ □ □ □

Innovation

29. Customers are always queried before we embark on
    product innovations. . . . . □ □ □ □ □

30. We target product innovations that customers
    strongly value. . . . . □ □ □ □ □

31. Innovation is a key organizational strategy. . . . . □ □ □ □ □

32. Innovations are never taken simply for the sake of
    innovation. . . . . □ □ □ □ □

33. Innovations are always validated prior to full market
    rollout. . . . . □ □ □ □ □

Organizational Culture

34. Employees are recognized for their contributions to
    excellent customer service. . . . . □ □ □ □ □

35. Employees at all levels have the authority to take
    action to ensure customer satisfaction. . . . . □ □ □ □ □

36. Our organization has a process for getting to know
    our customers personally . . . . □ □ □ □ □

37. We're focused on helping our customer become more
    successful. . . . . □ □ □ □ □

38. We have a systematic way of soliciting employee ideas for improving products, processes, and customer service. . . . . □ □ □ □ □

39. We always hire the kind of people who take charge and make customer satisfaction their personal responsibility. . . . . □ □ □ □ □

Training

40. Employee training includes how each person can affect the customer. . . . . □ □ □ □ □

41. Employees are trained in effective customer communication. . . . . □ □ □ □ □

42. Employee training stresses ethical behavior. . . . . □ □ □ □ □

43. Until they've received appropriate training, employees never come into contact with customers . . □ □ □ □ □

44. Our training programs are revised when we discover new and better methods for ensuring customer satisfaction. . . . . □ □ □ □ □

Management Systems

45. We take pains to keep our management system as streamlined as possible. . . . . □ □ □ □ □

46. We always try to utilize simple, visual procedures to control our processes. . . . . □ □ □ □ □

47. Responsibilities and authorities for serving customers are clearly defined at all levels of our organization. . . . .

48. We use a process matrix to define our processes and communicate how they're related. . . . .

49. We have a systematic way of capturing customer requirements. . . . .

50. Every process in our organization is linked to a customer. . . . .

Strongly agree −2 Disagree −1 Neutral 0 Agree 1 Strongly disagree 2

Total score: _____

Participants: _____

Date completed: _____

APPENDIX B

Customer Concerns Worksheet

Section 1

Completed by:_____ Date: _____
Name of organization: _____
Primary customer(s):_____
Primary products(s): _____

Section 2

2.1. Why do customers buy from us instead of our competitors? _____
_____
_____

2.2. What is one of the "little things" that customers really like about
us?_____
_____

2.3. If I had to sell a prospective customer with only one word, what
would it be? _____
_____

2.4. What was our biggest customer-service success last year? _____
_____

2.5. When customers think of us and smile, what are they thinking
about?_____
_____

Section 3

3.1. What was the top customer complaint of the last year? _____

_____

3.2. What's our biggest weakness in general? _____

_____

3.3. Day-in and day-out, what keeps us from serving customers? _____

_____

3.4. What makes customers the most frustrated? _____

_____

3.5. When customers are really depending on us, what do they worry about the most? _____

_____

Section 4

4.1. What direction is our industry and/or environment headed in? ____

_____

4.2. What do customers seem to want the most? _____

_____

4.3. What will make us (or keep us) the leader in the minds of our customers? _____

_____

4.4. What's our most promising opportunity for capturing new opportunities? _____

_____

Section 5

5.1. What changes current customers to former customers? _____

_____

5.2. Who's our biggest competitor? _____

_____

5.3. What do customers like about this competitor? _____

_____

5.4. What product or company, not currently competing against us, could go head-to-head with us in the future? _____

_____

5.5. Our biggest scare of the last year was: _____

_____

Section 6: Narrowing Our Focus

6.1. From section 2, what themes emerge? Select up to two issues from the customer themes worksheet: _____

_____

6.2. From section 3, what themes emerge? Select up to two issues from the customer themes worksheet: _____

_____

6.3. From section 4, what themes emerge? Select up to two issues from the customer themes worksheet: _____

_____

6.4. From section 5, what themes emerge? Select up to two issues from the customer themes worksheet: _____

_____

Section 7: Key Customer Concerns

Choose the five most important themes that emerged in section 6 and write them below.These will be the issues that your customer survey will focus upon.

7.1: _____

_____

_____

_____

7.2: _____

_____

_____

_____

7.3: _____

_____

_____

_____

7.4: _____

_____

_____

_____

7.5: _____

_____

_____

_____

Customer Themes Worksheet

- Accessibility
- Attractiveness
- Availability of goods and services
- Billing
- Cleanliness
- Communication
- Conformity
- Convenience
- Courtesy
- Delivery performance
- Design
- Discretion
- Durability
- Effectiveness
- Empathy
- Ethics
- Fun
- Helpfulness

- Innovation
- Knowledge
- Labeling
- Maintainability
- Packaging
- Performance
- Prestige
- Pricing
- Problem solving
- Professionalism
- Quotes
- Reliability
- Responsiveness
- Safety
- Sex appeal
- Style
- Technical support
- Value

Sample Survey Statements

M atch the issues below to the ones that appeared in section 7 of your customer concerns worksheet. Choose one statement in each applicable section, up to a total of five. These will be the statements that appear on your mini-survey.

All of these statements are in the present tense. If you plan to administer the survey soon after the consumption of the good or service, it's recommended that you change the statement into past tense to give a tone of immediacy. An example using the first statement below would be, "I was able to contact the organization when I needed to."

Accessibility

- I'm able to contact the organization when I need to.
- I never worry about reaching an employee.*
- Employees* are easy to get in touch with.
- It's easy to get in touch with the organization.
- I don't get put into voice mail.
- The company makes it easy to contact them.
- Personnel* are always on call when I need them.

---

* Consider customizing this word to match the person who's actually the subject of the statement. Examples include accountant, agent, analyst, auditor, clerk, consultant, coordinator, dispatcher, doctor, engineer, examiner, instructor, investigator, mechanic, model, nurse, officer, operator, planner, representative, scientist, specialist, teacher, and technician, among many others. The job title might need to be made plural or singular, depending on the structure of the survey statement.

** Consider customizing this word to match the specific product or service in question.

Attractiveness

- Products** supplied by this company always look good.
- The products** are appealing to the eyes.
- I like this company's products** because they're striking.
- Beautiful is a word I would use to describe these products.**
- I like to look at these products.**
- The personnel* are very attractive.

Availability of goods and services

- The lead times quoted to me are always adequate.
- Products** are rarely out of stock.
- The service** took place in the desired time frame
- The product and/or service** is always available when I need it.
- I can get products** when I need them.
- My operation has never shut down due to the unavailability of these products.**

Billing

- Invoices arrive when they're supposed to.
- Invoices are always accurate.
- I don't get frustrated by this company's billing process.
- I can understand all the details that appear on my invoice.
- I don't feel that the company tries to deceive me through confusing billing.

Cleanliness

- Cleanliness is something that the employees seem to care about very much.
- The facility is exceptionally clean.
- The employees* take pride in cleanliness.
- I never see litter or refuse on the grounds.
- The facility is among the cleanest I have seen.

Communication

- Communication with employees* is very clear.
- I always understand what's being said by employees.*

- Confusion never results from communication with employees.*
- It's easy to initiate communication with the organization.
- Talking with employees* is pleasant.
- Communication problems are quickly resolved with employees.*

Conformity

- The product** consistently meets our specifications.
- Product** tolerances are never exceeded.
- The product** is exactly what I ordered.
- The product** meets my requirements.
- The service was executed the way I wanted it.
- The company understands my requirements and always meets them.
- Quantities are always correct.
- Personnel* always perform consistently.

Convenience

- It's convenient to do business with this organization.
- Buying from this company is easy.
- Convenience is one of the key reasons I'm a customer.
- This company has locations where I need them.
- Employees* keep me from being inconvenienced.
- This organization operates with my convenience in mind.

Courtesy

- Representatives* always seem happy to talk to me.
- Rudeness is never an issue.
- I'm always greeted like an important customer.
- I'm consistently treated with the respect by employees.*
- Employees* never "talk down" to me.
- This organization makes me feel like a good friend.

Delivery performance

- The product arrives when it's supposed to.
- Late orders are a rare occurrence.
- I'm always notified if a delay is expected.
- The company consistently provides a product when it's promised.
- Delivery personnel are courteous.

Design

- The product works well for its intended application.
- This company designs excellent products.**
- Products** have the features I want.
- I'm impressed by the design of this company's products.**
- Products** are designed with the proper functionality.
- This company seems to read my mind when it designs a new product.**

Discretion

- My affairs are kept private by employees.*
- Nobody within the organization has ever betrayed my confidence.
- I don't hesitate to share information with employees* because I know they will guard it.
- The organization can be trusted with my valuable information.
- I trust the employees* with my personal information.
- My privacy is never in question when I do business with this organization.

Durability

- Products** supplied by this company are tough.
- Indestructible is a good description for these products.**
- I'm not afraid of wearing out these products.**
- I can confidently tackle any job with the products** supplied by this company.
- Products** I buy from this organization are very durable.

Effectiveness

- The products** do what they're supposed to do.
- Personnel* always get the job done.
- Service is consistently effective.
- This product works better than competing products.**
- This organization's personnel* are more effective than the competitors'.
- The product gets the job done.
- The personnel* are effective in assisting me.

Empathy

- I never feel that the company doesn't care about me.
- Employees* are "on my side."
- I feel that personnel* can relate to my difficulties.
- This organization knows what I have to go through.
- Employees* really care about me.

Ethics

- This organization is very ethical.
- I believe this company obeys all laws that apply to it.
- Ethics are a key value of this organization.
- Employees* uphold high ethical standards.
- I have no reason to believe that this company does anything wrong.

Fun

- I have fun when I come here.
- This place makes me smile.
- The employees* act like they want me to have a good time.
- Fun is a word I would use to describe my interactions with this company.
- I always leave here happy.
- It's not unusual for me to laugh when I'm a customer here.

Helpfulness

- Employees* are always interested in helping me.
- I never have to search for an employee* to help me.
- This company is dedicated to helping me be more successful.
- I always feel that I receive the proper help when I'm a customer.

Innovation

- This organization is always developing new and exciting products.**
- This company's products** are on the cutting edge.
- Competitors' products** are less innovative.
- I'm a trendsetter when I use these products.**
- Employees* think in innovative ways.
- This company is a trailblazer.

Knowledge

- Employees* always know what they're doing.
- Personnel* have a firm grasp of their jobs.
- I'm never faced with ignorant employees.*
- This company seems to make sure its employees* are well-trained.
- Employees* have the necessary knowledge to assist me.
- Employees* are very knowledgeable.

Labeling

- The product always arrives with the desired labeling.
- Product labeling is clear and readable.
- There's never any question about the identity of products** when they arrive.
- Labels don't fall off.
- The labeling is durable.

Maintainability

- The products** are easy to maintain.
- Maintenance isn't difficult.
- Spare parts are easy to obtain.
- These products** require less maintenance than competing products.**
- These products** require very little maintenance.

Packaging

- Packaging is well-suited to the product.**
- The products** never arrive damaged.
- Packaging materials are easy to recycle or dispose of.
- The product's** packaging facilitates its handling and movement.
- Packaging isn't excessive.

Performance and/or overall performance

- I'll purchase products ** from this organization in the future.
- I'd recommend this company to a friend.
- I'm very satisfied with the service** I receive from this company.
- I'm very satisfied with the performance of employees.*

- This organization is a model of how to serve customers.
- Employees* strive to meet all my needs.
- This company is dedicated to customer satisfaction.
- Employees* are dedicated to customer satisfaction.
- I plan to be a long-term customer of this organization.
- Doing business with this company is always a smart decision.
- The products** are world-class.
- The quality of personnel* is world-class.
- This company is the best in the industry.
- I'm proud to do business with this organization.
- The product and/or service** is effective in meeting my needs.

Prestige

- I'd rather be seen using one of this company's products.**
- Using this company's products** means I've achieved high status.
- People recognize that this organization represents the best available service.
- No other products** afford the prestige I gain when I use these products.**
- I feel better about myself when I use these products.**

Pricing

- Pricing of products** is fair.
- I consider product** pricing to be competitive.
- The price of services** matches the benefit I receive.
- The benefit I receive far outweighs the price I pay for these products.**

Problem solving

- Personnel* are able to identify the root causes of my problems.
- The organization is dedicated to effective problem solving.
- Prevention of problems is a core value of this company.
- When something goes wrong, employees* are quick to fix it.
- Personnel* have creative solutions for addressing problems.
- I have confidence in the problem-solving abilities of this company.

Professionalism

- Employees* conduct themselves professionally.
- Everybody I deal with has a polished manner.
- I feel like more of a professional when I deal with this organization.
- This company is more professional than its competitors.
- Professionalism is one of the core values of this organization.

Quotes

- Quotes are provided quickly.
- Quotes include all the information I need.
- The amount quoted rarely changes later during the project.
- I feel that the organization does a good job of quoting its services.**
- When I receive a quote, I'm confident that I know the exact cost.

Reliability

- I don't have to worry about these products** breaking down.
- Product** failures are rare.
- Repair is never an issue because these products** are so reliable.
- The reliability of these products** is one of their biggest strengths.
- Employees* are very reliable.

Responsiveness

- The company is very responsive to my needs.
- Employees* are very responsive to my needs.
- When a problem comes up, personnel* act quickly to address it.
- I'm always called back promptly.
- I feel that the organization responds well.
- Personnel* act quickly to address my needs.

Safety

- I feel safe when I use these products.**
- Using these products** doesn't pose unusual hazards to me.
- Instructions adequately cover safety features.
- Getting hurt isn't something I worry about when I use this prodct.**
- I've never been injured using this product.**
- I don't feel unsafe when I come to this place of business.

- I feel comfortable taking my family here.
- All necessary safety features come standard with the products.**
- Personnel* never act in an unsafe manner.

Sex appeal

- I feel sexy when I use this product.**
- Using this product** makes members of the opposite sex desire me more.
- This product** increases my sex appeal.
- The company knows how to incorporate sex appeal into its products.**
- Personnel* are always sexy.

Style

- Products** provided by this organization have a distinctive flair.
- I feel stylish when I use these products.**
- People know I'm very cool when they see me using these products.**
- This company sets the style in the industry.
- Personnel* are always stylish.

Technical support

- Technicians* know their products** inside and out.
- This organization makes sure its personnel* have the proper technical expertise.
- I'm impressed by the technical competence of employees.*
- Outstanding technical support is one of the reasons I'm a customer.
- Technical support is always effective.

Value

- The products** represent good value for the money.
- I feel like I get my money's worth when I do business with this organization.
- Buying from this company is a wise business decision.
- The cost of the services** is overshadowed by their value.
- The work of employees* is always a good value.
- Personnel* focus on things that really matter to our success.

APPENDIX E

Sample Survey Scales

Scale 1

The scale below is the one most commonly used for survey statements. It covers the full range of responses, has a logical flow, and is balanced.

1	2	3	4	5
Strongly disagree	Disagree	Neither agree nor disagree	Agree	Strongly agree

(The scale can also be reversed, so that strongly agree is shown first.)

Scale 2

This scale is a variation on scale one. It doesn't allow a "neutral" response, forcing the respondent to take a stand. This approach appeals to people who perceive a tendency for respondents to choose the middle point.

1	2	3	4
Strongly disagree	Disagree	Agree	Strongly agree

(The scale can also be reversed, so that strongly agree is shown first.)

Scale 3

This scale appeals to organizations that favor clear, unambiguous responses. Military organizations that utilize surveys often choose this scale because it keeps issues in black-and-white terms. A scale of this sort is almost always paired with the request, "If no, please explain."

1	2
No	Yes

(The scale can also be reversed, so that yes is shown first.)

New Product Proposal

Brief description of new product: _____
_____
(Attach additional documentation if necessary)
Proposed by: _____ Date: _____
Telephone: _____ E-mail: _____

Initial Analysis

1. Does the new product fit in an existing product line?
   ☐ Yes   ☐ No
   If yes, what product line?_____
   _____

2. Do we possess the production and/or service capability to deliver this new product?
   ☐ Yes   ☐ No
   If yes, what specific capabilities would be employed? _____
   _____

3. Do we possess the technical and/or engineering capabilities to develop this new product?
   ☐ Yes   ☐ No
   If yes, what specific capabilities would be employed? _____
   _____

4. Is the new product aimed at an existing customer segment for our organization?
   ☐ Yes   ☐ No
   If yes, what customer segment? _____
   _____

5. Does the new product fit our current strategy?

 If yes, what is the connection to current strategy? _____

 _____

6. Does the new product fill an existing need or desire?
 ☐ Yes   ☐ No
 If yes, what is the need or desire? _____

 _____

7. Would we be the first organization to fill this need or desire in this manner?
 ☐ Yes   ☐ No
 If no, who already addresses the need or desire in this general way?

 _____

8. Do our existing suppliers and subcontractors have the capability for this product?
 ☐ Yes   ☐ No
 If yes, who will be the key suppliers and subcontractors?_____

 _____

9. Do our sales partners (e.g., dealers, retailers, and sales representatives) have the capabilities to handle this product?
 ☐ Yes   ☐ No
 If yes, who will be the key sales partners? _____

 _____

10. Will the sales for this new product represent at least $100,000 during the first year?
 ☐ Yes   ☐ No
 If yes, what evidence indicates this level of sales? _____

 _____

11. Will sales of the new product grow by at least 15 percent during each of the first three years of the product's life?
    ☐ Yes   ☐ No
    If yes, what evidence indicates this level of sales? _____
    _____

12. Will customers for this product reside in geographical areas currently served by our organization?
    ☐ Yes   ☐ No
    If yes, where will the bulk of the customers reside? _____
    _____

13. Will this product represent a completely new innovation for the marketplace?
    ☐ Yes   ☐ No
    If yes, what makes it unique? _____
    _____

14. Do we have the time and resources to pursue this project effectively, given the existing load of projects and new product development already undertaken?
    ☐ Yes   ☐ No
    If yes, what projects could possibly impede progress anyway? _____
    _____

15. Additional issues related to this proposal: _____
    _____
    _____
    _____
    _____
    _____
    _____
    _____

(Attach documentation if necessary)

Score and Approval Guidance

The score is based on the total number of "yeses" from above:

Score	Guidance	Approvals needed to proceed to detailed market analysis
0–4	RED (danger, possible incompatibility, high risk)	CEO Vice president of innovation Director of sales
5–8	YELLOW (caution, moderate risk)	Vice president of innovation Director of sales
9–14	GREEN (attractive, favorable fit, synergies)	Director of sales

Approvals

Approved by	Title	Date

Approved by	Title	Date

Approved by	Title	Date

New product: _____

New product sponsor: _____

APPENDIX G

Detailed Market Analysis

New product no: _____ Sponsor: _____
Brief description: _____
_____
_____
Market analysis completed by: _____
Date started: _____ Date completed: _____
Customers selected for market analysis:

	Customer name	Rationale for selection	Contact person	Contact info (phone or e-mail)
1.				
2.				
3.				
4.				

Instructions for conducting customer new-product queries

1. Ask the contact if he or she can spare a few minutes completing the survey. It should take no more than five minutes.
2. Describe product concept to customer in detail, using the description documented on the new-product proposal.
3. Read each statement to the contact, asking him or her to respond using the scale provided.
4. Thank the customer for his or her time.

Customer 1

Customer name: _____   Contact person: _____

Date contacted: _____   Contacted by: _____

	Strongly agree	Disagree	Neutral	Agree	Strongly disagree
	1	2	3	4	5

1.1.   This product addresses our needs. .... ☐ ☐ ☐ ☐ ☐

1.2.   This product is unique. .... ☐ ☐ ☐ ☐ ☐

1.3.   We're likely to purchase this product. .... ☐ ☐ ☐ ☐ ☐

1.4.   This product will enable us to be more successful. .... ☐ ☐ ☐ ☐ ☐

1.5.   This product is superior to alternatives we have now. ☐ ☐ ☐ ☐ ☐

1.6.   Estimated purchasing volume of this product during the first year:

_____

1.7.   Special performance requirements: _____

_____

_____

1.8.   Special aesthetic requirements: _____

_____

_____

1.9.   Special delivery requirements: _____

_____

_____

1.10. What else is important for us to know about this new product?

_____

_____

Customer 2

Customer name: _____ Contact person: _____

Date contacted: _____ Contacted by: _____

	Strongly agree	Disagree	Neutral	Agree	Strongly disagree
	1	2	3	4	5

2.1. This product addresses our needs. .... ☐ ☐ ☐ ☐ ☐

2.2. This product is unique. .... ☐ ☐ ☐ ☐ ☐

2.3. We're likely to purchase this product. .... ☐ ☐ ☐ ☐ ☐

2.4. This product will enable us to be more successful. ... ☐ ☐ ☐ ☐ ☐

2.5. This product is superior to alternatives we have now. . ☐ ☐ ☐ ☐ ☐

2.6. Estimated purchasing volume of this product during the first year:

_____

2.7. Special performance requirements:_____

_____

_____

2.8. Special aesthetic requirements: _____

_____

_____

2.9. Special delivery requirements:_____

_____

_____

2.10. What else is important for us to know about this new product?

_____

_____

Customer 3

Customer name: _____   Contact person: _____

Date contacted: _____   Contacted by: _____

		Strongly agree	Disagree	Neutral	Agree	Strongly disagree
		1	2	3	4	5
3.1.	This product addresses our needs.	☐	☐	☐	☐	☐
3.2.	This product is unique.	☐	☐	☐	☐	☐
3.3.	We're likely to purchase this product.	☐	☐	☐	☐	☐
3.4.	This product will enable us to be more successful. ..	☐	☐	☐	☐	☐
3.5.	This product is superior to alternatives we have now. .	☐	☐	☐	☐	☐

3.6.   Estimated purchasing volume of this product during the first year:

_____

3.7.   Special performance requirements:_____

_____

_____

3.8.   Special aesthetic requirements: _____

_____

_____

3.9.   Special delivery requirements:_____

_____

_____

3.10. What else is important for us to know about this new product?

_____

_____

Customer 4

Customer name: _____ Contact person: _____
Date contacted: _____ Contacted by: _____

	Strongly agree	Disagree	Neutral	Agree	Strongly disagree
	1	2	3	4	5

4.1. This product addresses our needs. .... ☐ ☐ ☐ ☐ ☐

4.2. This product is unique. .... ☐ ☐ ☐ ☐ ☐

4.3. We're likely to purchase this product. .... ☐ ☐ ☐ ☐ ☐

4.4. This product will enable us to be more successful. ... ☐ ☐ ☐ ☐ ☐

4.5. This product is superior to alternatives we have now. . ☐ ☐ ☐ ☐ ☐

4.6. Estimated purchasing volume of this product during the first year:

_____

4.7. Special performance requirements:_____

_____

_____

4.8. Special aesthetic requirements: _____

_____

_____

4.9. Special delivery requirements:_____

_____

_____

4.10. What else is important for us to know about this new product?

_____

_____

Analysis

Average and median responses for questions 1–5

1. This product addresses our needs.

   Average:_____   Median: _____

2. This product is unique.

   Average:_____   Median: _____

3. We're likely to purchase this product.

   Average:_____   Median: _____

4. This product will enable us to be more successful.

   Average:_____   Median: _____

5. This product is superior to alternatives we have now.

   Average:_____   Median: _____

Themes and trends from questions 6–10

6a. Estimated purchasing volume of this product during the first year [average of all responses]: _____

   _____

6b. Estimated purchasing volume of this product during the first year [median of all responses]: _____

   _____

7. Special performance requirements:_____

   _____

8. Special aesthetic requirements:_____

   _____

9. Special delivery requirements: _____

   _____

10. What else is important for us to know about this new product?_____

   _____

Lowest average response to any question	Guidance	Approvals needed to proceed to inside/out review
1–2.9	RED (danger, low market acceptance, little perceived value or uniqueness)	CEO Vice president of innovation Director of sales
3–3.9	YELLOW (caution, moderate risk, uncertain market acceptance)	Vice president of innovation Director of sales
4–5	GREEN (attractive, favorable initial perceptions, market enthusiasm)	Director of sales

Approvals

Approved by   Title   Date

Approved by   Title   Date

Approved by   Title   Date

Inside/Out Review

New product No.: _____ Sponsor: _____

Brief description: _____

_____

_____

1. Business Analysis

What are the expected results of this new product?

| | Year 1 | Year 2 | Year 3 |

1.1. Number of units sold: Best case _____   _____   _____

Worst case _____   _____   _____

Units are: _____

1.2. Estimated product selling price:

Best case $/unit _____ $/unit _____ $/unit_____

Worst case $/unit _____ $/unit _____ $/unit_____

1.3. Estimated annual sales:

Best case $ _____ $ _____ $ _____

Worst case $ _____ $ _____ $ _____

1.4 How much capital investment:

Best case $ _____ $ _____ $ _____

Worst case $ _____ $ _____ $ _____

1.5. Estimated gross margin:

Best case % _____   % _____   % _____

Worst case % _____   % _____   % _____

1.6 Does this product have any other direct or indirect financial benefit?
☐ Yes ☐ No
If yes, what are the benefits?_____

_____

_____

_____

Business analysis performed by:

_____   _____   _____
Name   Title   Date

Reviewed by:

_____   _____
Business group manager   Date

2. Technical analysis

2.1. What are the performance specifications of this product? _____

_____

_____

(Attach documentation if necessary)

2.2. Does this product have tolerances that must be met? ☐ Yes ☐ No
If yes, what are the tolerances? _____

_____

_____

_____

2.3. Will any statutory or regulatory requirements affect this product in
any state or country in which it's likely to be sold? ☐ Yes ☐ No
If yes, what are the requirements?_____

_____

_____

_____

2.4. Is this product similar to previous designs that we've developed?
   ☐ Yes   ☐ No

   _____

   _____

   _____

   _____

2.5. What tests or trials are needed for the new product? _____

   _____

   _____

   _____

2.6. What equipment will be required to produce this product? _____

   _____

   _____

   _____

2.7. What competencies will be required of personnel to produce this product?
   Education: _____
   Training: _____

   _____

   Skills: _____

   _____

   Experience: _____

   _____

   _____

2.8. Is new technology required to produce this product?
   ☐ Yes   ☐ No
   If yes, what technology? _____

   _____

   What is the source of this technology? _____

   _____

2.9. Will this product have any significant impacts on the environment?
☐ Yes ☐ No
If yes, what impacts? _____

_____

2.10. How will this product be disposed of at the end of its life? _____

_____

_____

2.11. Will existing production or service be affected by this new product?
☐ Yes ☐ No
If yes, what are the effects? _____

_____

2.12. What additional production concerns relate to this new product? __

_____

_____

Technical analysis performed by:

_____   _____   _____
Name   Title   Date

Reviewed by:

_____   _____
Technical manager   Date

3. Marketing analysis

3.1. Who are the customers for this product? _____

_____

Are they ready to place orders? ☐ Yes ☐ No
On what evidence do you base this? _____

What are the initial quantities? _____

3.2. What is this product's relationship to our strategic core business? ___

3.3. Describe the specific target segment of customers: _____

_____

3.4. What is the projected growth rate of this market? _____

On what is this projection based? _____

3.5. Who are the current competitors for this product? _____

What are their strengths? _____

What are their weaknesses? _____

How will marketing use the knowledge of these strengths and weaknesses? _____

3.6. What specific marketing techniques will be most appropriate for this product? _____

3.7. What theme(s) will the marketing stress to make a lasting and favorable impression on customers?_____

_____

_____

3.8. What advertising media will be most appropriate for this product? _

_____

_____

3.9. Are there any known patents related to this product?
      ☐ Yes   ☐ No
      If yes, who holds the patent(s)? _____

_____

3.10. Is this product patentable?   ☐ Yes   ☐ No

3.11. Are there any real or potential liabilities related to this product (e.g., safety or legal)? _____

_____

_____

3.12. Will this new product affect any of our current products?
      ☐ Yes   ☐ No
      If yes, what products will be affected and what will be the effects?__

_____

_____

_____

3.13. What are the strategic consequences of not pursuing this idea? ____

_____

_____

Marketing analysis performed by:

_____   _____   _____
Name   Title   Date

Reviewed by:

_____   _____
Marketing and/or sales manager   Date

APPENDIX I

Customer Profile

Company Information

Company name: _____

Telephone: _____ Fax: _____

Billing address: _____

Shipping address: _____

Products purchased: _____

_____

Special requests, if any: _____

_____

_____

_____

_____

Open issues and/or complaints, if any:_____

_____

_____

_____

Primary customers: _____

_____

Product end-uses:_____

_____

_____

_____

_____

_____

_____

_____

Personal Information

Key contact person: _____ Title: _____

Telephone: _____ Fax: _____

E-mail: _____

Interests and hobbies: _____

_____

_____

_____

_____

_____

Spouse's name, if applicable:_____

Children's name(s), if applicable:_____

_____

Pets, if any: _____

Notes from last conversation:_____

_____

_____

_____

_____

_____

_____

_____

_____

_____

_____

_____

_____

_____

_____

_____

Last updated:_____ Updated by: _____

AFTERWORD

BellSouth Communications Systems LLC (BCS) specializes in provisioning voice and data communications equipment to BellSouth network customers as part of a total communications package. During the last few years, we've seen substantial growth in our VOIP and other data-centric applications. I attribute this growth to our ability to be a customer-focused organization during our transition to delivering converged communications solution. So what does this mean in real terms, and how does it relate to concepts discussed in this book?

First, our reputation as a best-in-class service provider in traditional voice solutions gave our customers the confidence to trust us with converged voice applications. Now the onus was on us to meet or exceed our customer expectations. To do so, we had to ensure that we had the people, processes, and systems in place as well as a timely feedback system to determine if we were meeting customer needs. Let's take a look at each of the elements we believe are essential to being a customer-focused organization.

- *People.* The number-one element is having the right people with the right skill sets. There are two ways to accomplish this. One way is to hire them. Another way—our preferred approach—is to train and certify our people in data competencies. In fact, both our equipment partners have certification requirements for us to be able to sell their products, and we work closely with them to achieve and maintain the necessary certifications.

- *Systems.* Our systems must be user-friendly. They must enable our people to provision orders from the initial quotation to final billing, and then transition to supporting and maintaining the customers' applications after the sale. Systems must have a back-end interface with our key suppliers to facilitate provisioning. In addition, they should give the customer the option to do business with us electronically if they so choose. During the last few years, we've made much progress in this area and are continuing along this path.

- *Processes.* Another key element is to have robust processes in place throughout the sales cycle to ensure that we can propose and implement timely and competitive solutions that meets customers' needs.
- *Customer feedback.* We use customer feedback from several customer satisfaction and loyalty surveys to drive corrective action and improve processes. This information is also relayed to our suppliers for product issues.
- *Performance metrics and accountability.* We make extensive use of balanced scorecards to hold our management teams accountable for meeting targets related to all of the above attributes.

In summary, being a customer-focused organization is a long and challenging journey that requires a total commitment and a robust plan. By staying the course, we've seen the rewards in increased employee engagement scores and higher customer satisfaction results, which in turn have generated increased revenues, productivity, and lower costs. Smart companies will seize the necessity of becoming truly customer focused. Craig Cochran's book provides an ideal road map for this journey.

—Danny Helmly
President and CEO, BellSouth Communications Systems LLC

Index

ABOUT THE AUTHOR

Craig Cochran is the North Metro Regional Manager with Georgia Tech's Economic Development Institute. He has an MBA from the University of Tennessee and a bachelor's degree in industrial management from the Georgia Institute of Technology. Cochran is a Certified Quality Manager, Certified Quality Engineer, and Certified Quality Auditor through the American Society for Quality. He's certified as a QMS Lead Auditor through the RABQSA.

Cochran writes and speaks extensively on management, improvement, problem solving, customer satisfaction, and quality. He's the author of *The Continual Improvement Process: From Strategy to the Bottom Line* and *Customer Satisfaction: Tools, Techniques, and Formulas for Success.*